# Cambridge Elements ⲻ

**Elements in Eighteenth-Century Connections**
edited by
Eve Tavor Bannet
*University of Oklahoma*
Markman Ellis
*Queen Mary University of London*

# LABOUR OF THE STITCH

## *The Making and Remaking of Fashionable Georgian Dress*

Serena Dyer
*De Montfort University*

Shaftesbury Road, Cambridge CB2 8EA, United Kingdom

One Liberty Plaza, 20th Floor, New York, NY 10006, USA

477 Williamstown Road, Port Melbourne, VIC 3207, Australia

314–321, 3rd Floor, Plot 3, Splendor Forum, Jasola District Centre, New Delhi – 110025, India

103 Penang Road, #05–06/07, Visioncrest Commercial, Singapore 238467

Cambridge University Press is part of Cambridge University Press & Assessment, a department of the University of Cambridge.

We share the University's mission to contribute to society through the pursuit of education, learning and research at the highest international levels of excellence.

www.cambridge.org
Information on this title: www.cambridge.org/9781009507493

DOI: 10.1017/9781009177689

When citing this work, please include a reference to the DOI 10.1017/9781009177689

First published 2024

A catalogue record for this publication is available from the British Library.

ISBN 978-1-009-50749-3 Hardback
ISBN 978-1-009-17769-6 Paperback
ISSN 2632-5578 (online)
ISSN 2632-556X (print)

Additional resources for this publication at www.cambridge.org/Dyer

# Labour of the Stitch

## The Making and Remaking of Fashionable Georgian Dress

Elements in Eighteenth-Century Connections

DOI: 10.1017/9781009177689
First published online: March 2024

Serena Dyer
*De Montfort University*

**Author for correspondence:** Serena Dyer, serena.dyer@dmu.ac.uk

**Abstract:** The making of fashionable women's dress in Georgian England necessitated an inordinate amount of manual labour. From the mantuamakers and seamstresses who wrought lengths of silk and linen into garments, to the artists and engravers who disseminated and immortalised the resulting outfits in print and on paper, Georgian garments were the products of many busy hands. This Element centres the sartorial hand as a point of connection across the trades which generated fashionable dress in the eighteenth century. Crucially, it engages with recreation methodologies to explore how the agency and skill of the stitching hand can inform understandings of craft, industry, gender, and labour in the eighteenth century. The labour of stitching, along with printmaking, drawing, and painting, composed a comprehensive culture of making and manual labour which, together, constructed eighteenth-century cultures of fashionable dress.

**Keywords:** Fashion history, recreative practice, material culture, sewing, making.

ISBNs: 9781009507493 (HB), 9781009177696 (PB), 9781009177689 (OC)
ISSNs: 2632-5578 (online), 2632-556X (print)

# Contents

## 1 Introduction

Hands made clothes in the eighteenth century. Each seam demanded that the sewer repeated the same steps. Fingers would snip a length of thread, run it through a block of wax, then deftly insert the tip of the thread through the eye of a needle. To prepare for the next task, the middle finger on the dominant hand would don a metal thimble – the only protection provided to the hand through this process of manufacture – before the sewer plied that needle up and down through the garment in production.[1] The sewing project at hand had been cut out with scissors and pinned into place. This small array of tools – needles, pins, scissors, thimble, and wax – was the sole occupant of an eighteenth-century sewing box (Beaudry, 2006). To the modern sewer, it is an astonishing dearth of implements. To anyone familiar with commercialised and mechanised cultures of sewing, involving sewing machines, overlockers, paper patterns, and an army of tiny sewing tools, or the industrial scale of the modern garment workshop, the relative reliance of the eighteenth-century sewer on their hands is remarkable. Every extravagant silk gown, each petticoat, and all shifts, whether they clothed the backs of royalty or the poor, were constructed the same way: by hand.

Women of the eighteenth century were materially creative and expert at turning their hands to making activities. Whether they laboured for a pittance as seamstresses or picked up their needles in moments of pleasurable leisure, women's sartorial handwork was ingenious, inventive, and resourceful. As Beth Fowkes Tobin and Maureen Daly Goggin have argued, eighteenth-century women's 'engagement with the material world [is] most obvious when a woman is making something' (2009, p. 2). For many historical women, the remnants of their lives remain only in the things they made (Dyer, 2021). Women's engagement with the material world around them was dynamic and skilled. Accessing, reading, and deciphering the imprint of women's material endeavours on the objects they made, while often challenging, offers a uniquely fruitful opportunity to appreciate how women of the past understood and engaged with the material world around them. This Element seeks to recover the skill and creativity of eighteenth-century women's sartorial handwork and, in so doing, positions histories of making as a crucial means of understanding the sensory, bodily, and manual practices of the past.

Confined to the backrooms of mantuamakers' shops, genteel parlours, and the humble dwellings of the poor, the dexterous hands of women's garment makers – both professional and amateur – have been historically overlooked,

---

[1] Sewer is used here as a term to refer to all hands that sewed, irrespective of their specialism, time period, professional or amateur status, or gender. It also encompasses all the elements of sewing, not just stitching, but is specific to sartorial labour as opposed to general making.

or worse, scorned as unskilled and insignificant (Haru Crowston, 2001; Hill, 2005; Simonton, 2018; Inder, 2020). This dismissal, the blame for which lies with a range of factors, from gendered struggles with the tailoring trades to broader issues around the framing of women's labour, has cast the manual skill of women's garment making into the shadows of the grand historical narratives which have dominated the study of eighteenth-century England, most notably, industrialisation (Bendall, 2021b; Bendall, 2022; Parker, 2010; Smith, 2013). During the later eighteenth century, the scenery of England altered radically. England's rolling hills and agricultural landscape became peppered with smoke-puffing factories, and its cities grew exponentially (Allen, 2009). By 1811, London's population was double what it had been at the start of the eighteenth century (Schwarz, 1992, pp. 125–128). The behemoth that was urbanised, industrialised England drew focus to the industrial innovation alongside the global trade of textiles. Cotton became 'the most traded of consumer goods in the world' (Riello, 2013, p. 266). Meanwhile innovations such as knitting frames and the spinning jenny, 'eliminat[ed] the need for the spinner's fingers' (Styles, 2020, p. 196). The industrialisation of textile manufacture actively aimed to reduce the necessity for hands within production processes, as inventors attempted to replicate and imitate the skill of the hand in mechanised form. As the nineteenth century progressed, the hands of garment makers would unevenly follow those of spinners and weavers, as the invention of the sewing machine gradually recast the role of haptic skill within the sewing process.

The progressive clamour towards industrialisation may have begun to subsume the production of textiles by the mid-eighteenth century, but the transformation of those textiles into garments continued to be a manual, haptic, and handcrafted process into the nineteenth century. The sewing machine's development, from invention in the 1790s, to commercialisation in the 1850s, and final dominance by 1900 was surprisingly slow (Gardner, 2019; Abrams and Gardner, 2021). Many garments from throughout the latter half of the nineteenth century, supposedly the heyday of the sewing machine's growth, only had their long construction seams stitched by machine.[2] Everything else from buttonholes to hems was completed by hand. The restrictions of machinery, and its limitation to repetitive perfunctory tasks, could not supplant the flexibility and responsiveness of the hand. As Peter Dormer argued, it is not the case that 'ever-improving technology replaces craft' (1997, p. 3). Hands could not yet be usurped.

---

[2] This has been observed from extensive examination of garments in the collections of the Fashion Museum, Bath; Killerton House, Exeter; Snowshill Manor, Gloucester; Leeds Museums and Galleries, among many others.

The eighteenth century played host to an increasingly industrial manufacturing culture. From the pottery of Josiah Wedgewood to the metalware of Matthew Bolton and the furniture of Thomas Chippendale, England's genteel and aristocratic homes were filled with manufactured fashionable goods fronted by the enterprising talents of powerful male designers and entrepreneurs (Vickery, 2009). Workshops and factories around the country fuelled a consumer desire for fashionable commodities. Yet, amidst this hungry manufacturing culture, fashion followed a different course. Fashion was never a finished product. The fabric held the monetary value, while the garment itself would be made and remade (Dowdell, 2017, p. 1). Unlike a vase or a chair, each garment was in a constant state of flux. It was adapted to fit a changing body, or evolving fashions, as sewing hands deftly oversaw each juncture of transformation. Garments in the eighteenth century, as was consistently the case until the later twentieth century, constantly underwent care and maintenance, making and remaking.

Stitching was not the only way in which cultures of fashion continued to be constructed by hand. Hands, too, produced the representations and reflections upon what was fashionable about that clothing. Through fashion plates – the engraved images of fashionable dress which grew to dominate women's periodicals – these fashions were delineated and disseminated (Smith 2018; Dyer, 2022). Hands lifted pencil to paper to sketch out each image, before picking up a burin – a wooden handled engraving tool – to incise the drawing onto the polished surface of a metal plate ready for printing (Stijnman, 2012). Building on the costume prints which circulated in early modern Europe, these images of fashionable dress first appeared in pocket books, which were small diaries and accounting books popular from the mid-century. These early fashion plates were small (approximately 8 cm by 13 cm), monochrome, and published annually. By the 1790s, fashion plate publishers had grown in scale and ambition. Now appearing in monthly periodicals, like Nicolaus Heideloff's *Gallery of Fashion* (1794–1802), the fashion plates were large (approximately 34 cm by 26 cm), hand-coloured, and depicted the fashions of the previous month, rather than the previous year (Figure 1).

This Element argues that hands offered the linkage across cultures of fashion, and yet their skill is often oblique.[3] Encountering elaborate gowns and appealing fashion plates often elicits distance between the modern-day observer and the skill of the maker. Those who are not themselves makers often either see the production process as mystical and elusive, or never consider it at all: the object

---

[3] Fashion, throughout this Element, refers to styles of dress which are temporally and culturally constructed.

**Figure 1** Fashion engraving, *Gallery of Fashion*, 1799, Metropolitan Museum of Art, New York, 50.611.1(5).

simply is. This Element interrogates this lacuna between maker and observer/ scholar both through an object-based examination of the products of this making, and through turning to recreative and embodied methods to autoethno-graphically explore ways in which the hand skills, which are otherwise absent from the historical record, might be rescued and restored. Recreation methods recentre attention on the vitality of the maker's hand and, as will be explained in Section 3, offer opportunities to comprehend making practice and its cultural resonances beyond the constraints of textual evidence. In so doing, the connections wrought by hands across sartorial cultures will be elucidated, and the labour of fashion reconnected to its bodily performance.

## 1.1 By Hand

The hand possessed artisanal supremacy in the making of fashion in the eighteenth century. That is not to say that the hand acted in isolation. Stitching was an experience that encompassed the whole body, as was the wearing of clothes. However, the hand carried a certain primacy as the vital point of haptic interaction with the garment in progress, and as the wielder of scissors, needles, and thimbles. The hand did not act alone, but its status as a tool for sartorial construction singles it out as worthy of focused study. The activities that human hands carry out are inherently located in a specific time and place. Changes in cutlery influenced how people used their hands to eat, while developments in technology have introduced swiping, pinching, and scrolling hand motions to the manual lexicon (Leader, 2017, p. 2). Eighteenth-century hands were no different. Their gestures, movement, and habits were shaped by that historical moment.[4] The sewing hand of the eighteenth century is not the same as that of the nineteenth century, supplemented by tools and machinery. Neither is it the same as the medieval hand, which was used to the sensation of different weaves and qualities of textile. The experience of sewing is haptically distinct to its time and place.

Hands, as Kate Smith has shown, were central to self-fashioning and meaning making, as well as practices of shopping, for genteel women of the eighteenth century (Smith, 2012; Smith, 2014). As Smith has stated, 'the hand existed with the card table, the teapot and the glove as a set of 'things' employed by genteel women keen to assert their awareness of fashion and their membership to a particular social group' (Smith, 2014, p. 438). Hands were something which were performed with, but the genteel, white hand's abstinence from manual labour was merely a part of the performance, and not a bodily reality. Creams and powders were concocted to exaggerate the whiteness and softness desired, while the hands that wore such lotions were often also the hands that made them (Smith, 2014, p. 492).[5] However, hands did also reflect aspects of labour. The hands of a mantuamaker who stitches for her bread and butter will be hardened

---

[4] On gestures in the eighteenth century, see, for example, Jan Bremmer and Herman Roodenburg (eds.), *A Cultural History of Gestures: From Antiquity to the Present* (Cambridge, 1991); Karen Harvey (ed.), *The Kiss in History* (Manchester, 2005); Colin Jones, *The Smile Revolution in Eighteenth-Century Paris* (Oxford, 2014).

[5] The fashion for whiteness was highly racialised. See, for example, Angela Rosenthal, "Visceral Culture: Blushing and the Legibility of Whiteness in Eighteenth-Century British Portraiture," *Art History* 27, no. 4 (2004): 563–92; Amina Mire, *Wellness in Whiteness: Biomedicalization and the Promotion of Whiteness and Youth Among Women* (London: Routledge, 2019).

by the work, while a genteel lady who stitches as she pleases may heal at her leisure before she lifts her needle again.

As signifiers, hands indicate agency and control. Hands move the strings of the puppet and grasp at objects desired by their wielders (Leader, 2017, pp. 6–7). They are also the most important tools of the crafter (Frye, 2011, p. 138). Glenn Adamson has argued that the industrial revolution developed parallel with craft (Adamson, 2013, p. xiii). Craft exists as industry's opposite. It is what mass production and mechanised manufacture are not. This bifurcation is felt through the binaries engaged with in this text. The consumer/producer binary, which I have written about elsewhere, is one of these many splits constructed to support a capitalist agenda of consumerist approaches to material goods (Dyer, 2021). Restored as the makers of fashion in the eighteenth century, hands challenge the binaries constructed to support economies of manufacture. Yet how their knowledge is accessed poses a challenge. While there were contemporary attempts to capture in writing the otherwise tacit knowledge of making, garment construction is largely absent from instructional manuals until the turn of the nineteenth century (Smith, Meyers and Cook, 2017; Smith, 2022). That vast knowledge was held within the maker's hands.

## 1.2 Recreative Methods

If we are to grasp the tacit knowledge wielded by the maker's hands, which is absent from the archival record and yet so culturally ubiquitous, then we must apply our own hands. Making as a means to know offers a phenomenological route to understanding the complex ways in which sartorial labour was experienced, understood, and impacted upon sartorial culture (Thomas, 2006; Smith et al., 2017; Smith, 2022). If the sartorial hand was cognisant, then these embodied approaches allow us to capture the complexities incumbent upon that hand. The possibilities of making as a methodology through which the past may be better understood have long been acknowledged in the field of archaeology, where Iron Age houses and medieval spoons have been created to test out theories and query concepts. Experimental archaeology is heavily rooted in the scientific method, as it 'tries to interpret the material culture, technology or ways of living in the past through scientific experiments' (Callaghan, 1999, p. 4). As Hilary Davidson has suggested, experimental *history* is equally valid as an approach, as historians endeavour to capture the fragments of material skill and knowledge which have been eroded by the passage of time (Davidson, 2019, p. 339). While experimental archaeologists work with fragments from the earth to piece back together how the people and objects of the past may have worked, experimental historians look to fill the inevitable gaps in the archival and material record left through the privileged and limited practices of record-ing and retaining records.

There has undoubtedly been, as Davidson has suggested, an 'embodied turn' in historical approaches to making knowledge, especially in histories of dress (Davidson, 2019, p. 352). Scholars such as Sarah Bendall, Jane Malcolm Davies, and Davidson have all deftly demonstrated how plying their own needles can deepen understanding of textiles, bodies, and fashion cultures of the past (Bendall, 2019; Malcolm-Davies et al., 2018; Davidson, 2015). Projects such as Pamela H. Smith's 'Making and Knowing Project' (Columbia University) and Paula Hohti's 'Refashioning the Renaissance' (Aalto University) have also deepened historians' engagement with making as a valid approach to the study of history, whether examining textiles, metalwork, or chemical experiments. Beyond histories of fashion and bodily adornment, Helen Williams has worked on recreative approaches to the history of type, and a team of curatorial and making experts have explored the recreation of eighteenth-century ceramics methods through the 'Making London Porcelain' project (Burgio et al., 2023).[6] Yet this remains a nascent area of study in History as a discipline. Terminologies, methods, and approaches are diverse, and tend to be fluidly moulded to fit individual projects' preoccupations.[7] Diversity of approaches is, of course, not a criticism. Methodological flexibility, especially in these early stages of the 'embodied turn', is necessary as scholars push the boundaries of what making can achieve for historians.

This Element explores how these recreative, embodied methods can elucidate on the labour, skill, and abilities of the sartorial hand, specifically in relation to the making of fashionable garments in the eighteenth century. An English gown (this terminology will be explained in depth in Section 2), the most ubiquitous of fashionable gown styles of the eighteenth century, will be recreated following methods gleaned from object-based research, as well as the processes used by other experimental historians. This recreation demonstrates the variety of skill enacted by the hands as a length of fabric was cut and stitched into a garment, as well as the logic, efficiency, and innovation expressed by the maker's hand. Finally, the process of dressing the body in the garment will be demonstrated, to reveal the parallels between sewing and dressing.

The methods employed here are inherently embodied and loosely phenom-enological. The fully embodied experience of sewing in the eighteenth century is all but impossible to capture. A recreative practitioner has neither the

---

[6] Helen Williams ran *Communicating Women's Work in the Historical Archive*, funded by the British Academy (2022-2023).

[7] My own AHRC network, *Making Historical Dress* (De Montfort University, 2023–2025), aims to tackle some of these issues.

environmental nor cultural experiences of an eighteenth-century sewer. Sewing while wearing eighteenth-century dress, while not attempted here, can add a level of experiential embodiment which would be productive to enquiries into, for example, the sewers' posture.[8] Sewing was, and continues to be, a holistic full-body experience. Hands carried out work supported by arms and elbows, backs and necks. Wearing contemporary stays and petticoats alters the sitting position and supports posture in a way which modern garments do not (Bendall, 2021a). However, there was no universal eighteenth-century experience. Different makers had nuanced and personal experiences of space, sewing, and their own bodies. Here, therefore, the focus is consciously upon the movement, skill, and practice of the hands. Sarah Woodyard, in her recreative work around the skills of the eighteenth-century milliner, referred to her process as a 'reflexive auto-ethnographic' methodology, which was 'sensorial and embodied' (Woodyard, 2017, p. 1). Similarly, this project will engage auto-ethnographically with the construction process, focusing on the movement and practice of the hands. The sensoriality of the haptics of sewing will be reflected upon, and the scientific methods of experimentation married with the experiential reflexivity of autoethnography.

Terminology around experimental history must be used deliberately. As Davidson has outlined, a plethora of terms, from reconstruction to replication, have been used by those engaging in making as a historical methodology (Davidson, 2019, pp. 337–338). Bendall and I have suggested 'historically informed sewing practice', while Woodyard has termed her methodology as 'hand sewn inquiry' (Woodyard, 2017).[9] Here, recreation is the most appropriate. The experimental process undertaken here does not aim to precisely replicate a garment in a museum collection; instead, it aims to create again (to re-create) the process of making such a garment. The techniques, methods, and processes evidenced in extant examples are, while rarely identical, parallel and comparable enough to extract a construction practice which is representative of how such a gown could have been made. The recreation process does not attempt to retrace the path of a specific pair of hands, but rather follows the shadows and echoes of the movements of multiple hands which laboured on gowns. Working under variable conditions, those hands did not homogeneously and unvaryingly churn out identical garments. They worked responsively and idiosyncratically,

---

[8] For a project which did engage with the experiential embodiment of the making process, see Carolyn Dowdell, "The Fruits of Nimble Fingers: Garment Construction and the Working Lives of Eighteenth-Century English Needlewomen" (MA, University of Alberta, 2010).

[9] The terminological approach of Bendall and myself is a product of our AHRC-funded network, *Making Historical Dress* (De Montfort University, 2023–2025).

following a consistent pattern of work, but with creative deviation born of preference, experience, and skill.

The practical heterogeneity of sewing practice leads us back to the relationship between industrialisation and the body. The responsiveness and creativity of the sewing hand, the needs of the body it clothed, and the uniformity necessitated by industrial manufacture were fundamentally at odds. Studies of eighteenth-century textile trade and manufacture have prized technological innovation and rightfully elevated its significance in social and economic histories of dress and textiles (Lemire, 1991; Riello and Roy, 2009; Riello, 2013; Styles, 2020; Miller, 2014). However, alongside these industrial histories, we must balance the histories of the industrious hands which transformed silks from Spitalfields and Lyon and cottons from India into the garments which clothed fashionable Georgian society. The economic and social appeal and power of these fabrics was established and displayed through their wear, and that wear was impossible without the labour of the sartorial hand.

## 1.3 Manual Labour of Fashion

Historians of fashion in the twentieth century onwards speak of 'fashion makers' (Walz and Morris, 1978). To them, the makers of fashion are the designers, leaders, and influencers whose impact stimulates and sets fashion. This concept is anachronistic to the eighteenth century, but it is a useful lens through which to consider by whom and how fashion was made and remade in the period. Without a fashion system comparable to the modern catwalks and design houses, fashion was both literally and conceptually made by the hands discussed in this Element. Figures like French modiste to Marie Antoinette, Rose Bertin, and Georgiana Cavendish, Duchess of Devonshire, who have been identified as leaders and innovators in fashion, were the outliers and not the core engine of fashion (Haru Crowston, 2001; Chrisman-Campbell, 2015). The focus on the haptic and manual undertaken in this Element also seeks to redress balance of agency and sartorial power between elite women and the makers responsible for the fashions which enhanced their fame. Fashion-maker-type characters appeared in fashion periodicals later in the period, such as Margaret Lanchester and Mary Ann Bell, who are credited as the minds behind the fashion plates. Bell is framed as the 'inventress' of the fashions depicted in the 1810s and 1820s, and she also ran millinery and dressmaking businesses in London (Batchelor, 2022, p. 119). But sixty years prior, fashions were invented and constructed in a collaborative process between client and maker; if, indeed, the client was not themselves also the maker (Dyer, 2020). The making of fashion was centred on these moments of manual labour: the cutting of the gown on the body, the stitching of the garment, dressing the body in the garment, and the drawing and engraving of fashion plates depicting those garments. In the eighteenth century, fashion was not an abstract network of trend setters and designers; fashion was the labour of the stitch, the pin, the scissors, the pencil, and the burin.

This Element is attentive to manual labour in a way which reflects eighteenth-century attitudes to the material world. Material literacy – meaning the understanding of the man-made material world, its materials, modes of making, and use of objects – was ever present in eighteenth-century cultures of production and consumption (Smith, 2012, 2014; Dyer and Smith, 2020). Eighteenth-century women, whether aristocratic, genteel, professional, or labouring, would have a fundamental understanding of how their garments were made. Although they may not all have excelled at needlework, it would be unusual for a woman not to have used a needle and thread. That is not to say that men were not also proficient with their needles (Harvey, 2016). However, the association between women and needlework – of both the decorative and practical varieties – was ubiquitous. That this was classed as labour – a term which will be critically returned to throughout the Element – was loaded with cultural meaning. Labour was both a derogatory term separating monotonous toil from expert skill, as well as a byword for industrious productivity (Kidwell, 1979, p. 3).

This Element considers cultures of fashionable dress in England in the long eighteenth century, with a particular focus on the mid-century decades. The 1750s to 1770s were pivotal to the development of cultures of fashion. By the 1770s, the circulation of fashion news in newspapers as well as periodicals would irreversibly speed up the temporalities of fashion (Dyer, 2022). Earlier in the century, the fundamentals of gown construction were still in flux, as the English gown evolved out of the mantua, a process which will be elaborated on in Section 2. This Element also focuses primarily on genteel cultures of fashion.[10] Poorer people engaged in and produced their own cultures of fashion (Styles, 2007). However, their garments were often second-hand and remade from genteel fashions of earlier years. While those moments of remaking are peripherally relevant to the Element, its primary focus is on the initial eighteenth-century process of making, and how remaking in the twenty-first century can illuminate that practice. The focus on England – and often London – is informed both by London's centrality to the periodical press, as well as an acknowledgement of regional differences. French man-tuamakers, for example, worked in a different system to those in England

---

[10]  Genteel is used here as outlined in Vickery (1998).

(Haru Crowston, 2001). Many of the arguments made in this Element will have wider relevance to cultures of fashion in Scotland, Wales, and Ireland, as well as across Europe and America.

Fashionable dress must be understood before it can be restitched, and stitched before it can be captured in ink and disseminated. This Element is therefore structured into this introductory section, followed by three subsequent sections. In 'Stitched Dress', the various styles, types, and terminology used to discuss women's dress in the eighteenth century will be outlined. This foundational knowledge will provide context as the section proceeds to discuss the variety of makers and their skills, unpicking the binaries of 'amateur'/'professional', 'good'/'poor' and 'skilled'/'unskilled'. Having established the variety of makers whose hands worked on garments, 'Recreating the English Gown' will offer an explanation and autoethnographic exploration of the recreation of a ubiquitous style of gown from the eighteenth century. This will conclude with an examination of how the garment was worn upon the body. The garment now united with its wearer, 'The Manual Labour of Style' will consider the connections between the labour of garment making and the broader labour of fashion production. It will reflect upon the myriad ways in which hands painted, engraved, wrote about, and otherwise wrought sartorial style in Georgian England, as well as how sartorially engaged women used their hands to creatively respond to, navigate, and engage with cultures of fashion. The Element will end with a reflection on the ways in which eighteenth-century cultures of fashionable dress rested upon and were joined together by the manual labours of the hand. In approaching dress through the embodied processes of labour, this Element looks beyond industrial and commercial rhetoric, and instead reveals a nuanced sartorial culture of hand labour.

## 2 Stitched Dress

Sartorial literacy in the eighteenth century was ubiquitous. Knowledge of garment making was not confined to the trades of mantuamakers and tailors. It permeated society, through both the witnessing and enactment of making. Both rich and poor alike stitched at home to make and mend clothing, while those who had no skill with the needle intimately participated in the making or adaptation of garments to fit their own bodies. While the ready-made market was expanding, most clothing continued to be either built for or adapted to the wearer's body (Lemire, 1984; Styles, 1994). However, the terminology and typologies of dress were, if not fluid, at least unstable. Historians, concerned with taxonomy and classification, have often struggled to define sartorial terms which, even to a contemporary eye, might have been variable dependent on place, time, and generational or cultural shifts (Buck, 1979; Ribeiro, 1985). Just as in modern-day regional Britain, a bread roll might also be termed a bap or a cob, dependent on localised vocabularies, in eighteenth-century England, the same garment might have been designated by a variety of different names. Terms once widely accepted amongst scholars of dress have since been revised and reinterpreted, and the creativity, commercialisation, and innovation of the later decades of the century certainly compounded this terminological quagmire (Van Cleave and Welborn, 2013). The fluidity of the sartorial lexicon amplifies the importance of the historian's material understanding. Haptic knowledge was infinitely more stable than language and labels, and tensions between text and object are ever-present.

This section begins with an outline of the contours of fashionable dress through the eighteenth century, touching on its evolutions and features, with the intent of providing a primer to those unfamiliar with key terms and the minutia of sartorial shifts. Having established what garments were made, the section will proceed to summarise where, when, and by whom fashionable dress was constructed in the eighteenth century. As well as professional mantua-makers, staymakers, tailors, milliners, and seamstresses (each of whom gener-ally constructed different elements of women's dress), this section will also consider the amateur hands which learnt to stitch garments for themselves. Crucially, this approach will avoid the pitfalls of binary distinctions between professional and amateur and men's and women's hands, often called upon as a marker of 'good'/'poor' and 'skilled'/'unskilled' construction by historians of the dressmaking trades. The hands which stitched these gowns possessed varied levels of skill, training, time, and dedication. Manual skill, this section shows, was a nuanced ability, which existed alongside and beyond imposed capitalist structures of professional labour. Dexterity with the needle was widespread and uneven in its distribution amongst makers.

## 2.1 The Ancestry and Evolution of the English Gown

As the seventeenth century rolled into the eighteenth, one of the most important shifts in the history of English fashion production occurred. This radical change was caused by the introduction of a new garment – the mantua – and the emergence of a new profession to construct it – the mantuamaker (Bendall, 2021b; Taylor, 2020; Birt, 2021; Earl, 1989). In 1688, Randle Holme described this garment as a 'loose Garment without, and Stiffe Bodies under them [ ... ] a great fashion for women [ ... ] some called them Mantuas' (Holme, 1688, III, 2, p. 19). The mantua was originally a T-shaped garment, with the sleeves usually cut in one with the body, and it was worn over heavily boned stays: the

'Stiffe Bodies' referenced by Holme.[11] It was this fundamental feature – the geometric and simple way in which the garment was cut – which set in motion a major shift in the professional gender segregation of sartorial labour. Prior to the 1670s, there had been a 'tailoring monopoly', as Bendall has termed it, over the production of women's gowns, stays, and outer garments (Bendall, 2021b, p. 38). Tailors, usually men, cut and constructed the elaborate gowns fashionable in the 1660s (Figure 2). Such garments required proficiency in careful fitting to the body, as well as complex construction, and such skills were perceived as artisanal and were economically valued (Bendall, 2021a, p. 143). Women garment makers had typically been seamstresses, who worked primarily with linen to stitch shirts, smocks, and shifts, as well as other linen items like aprons.[12] These items had one thing in common, like the mantua, they were cut from simple geometric shapes: squares, rectangles, and occasional triangles. Seamstresses were skilled with their needles, but the expertise of cutting

**Figure 2** Bodice, 1660s, Victoria and Albert Museum, 429-1889.

---

[11] This garment, the predecessor to the corset, was known as bodies in the seventeenth century, stays in the eighteenth century, and finally the corset in the nineteenth century.

[12] Women's under layers were known as smocks in the sixteenth century. This transitioned to shift by the eighteenth century.

complex curves to the body was confined to tailoring.[13] *Tailleur* in Old French literally meant 'one that cuts', and it was this skill in cutting out complex shapes which originally defined the tailoring trade. Tailoring, a guild-run profession, rarely admitted women as apprentices, although women often worked alongside male relatives (Inder, 2020, p. 15; Birt, 2021). By the middle of the eighteenth century, this gendered professional division of construction was fundamentally altered.

It is unclear whether the first swathe of mantuamakers in England were ambitious seamstresses or the wives and daughters of tailors (Inder, 2020, p. 16). Some may have been trained by French couturiers, while others made mantuas 'alongside tailors, and eventually without them' (Bendall, 2022, p. 394). As Bendall states, 'we know substantially more about the meanings of dress than we do about those who made it' (2021b, p. 24). This transitional period is fluid and foggy, especially in terms of trade titles. Bendall's verb and noun approach reveals that far more mantuamaking labour was being under-taken outside of structured trades. However, by 1700, mantuamakers had emerged as a distinct trade, initially set up to construct these simple T-shaped gowns, but soon constructing their more elaborate descendants. By the early decades of the eighteenth century, the mantua had evolved significantly. The once decorously flowing robe now clung to the body in deep pleats, which followed the fashionably long line of the torso (Figure 3). The side seams were now shaped to fit the body, and the sleeves cut separately and gently shaped. The voluminous skirts were elegantly pleated up to a belt around the waist and cascaded down into a train. The front closed over a stomacher, which was a simple stretched and truncated triangular piece of fabric, which filled the gap at the front of the mantua and concealed the separated stays beneath. This garment was the ancestor of all eighteenth-century gown styles, and its core construction methods would dominate women's fashionable dress for a century.

The mantua sits at the top of a family tree of garment styles that were gestated throughout the century. While the mantua persisted as a form of court dress throughout the century, its progeny dominated everyday fashionable dress (Greig, 2015; Dyer, 2020). Early offspring included the robe volante (Figure 4), which was customarily closed at the front of the skirts, leaving only the stomacher portion open (Haru Crowston, 2001, p. 41). The skirts, like the mantua, were cut all in one with the body, but they hung loosely away from the wearer to form an unstructured tent-like silhouette. The back fell in four box pleats from the neck, which loosely draped down the back to the floor. Like the early mantua, this gown was geometrically cut, with the back and front cut in

---

[13] Although, as Bendall has highlighted, some women worked outside this gendered binary to make tailored garments like waistcoats and bodiced gowns. See Bendall, 2022, pp. 402–408.

**Figure 3** Mantua, back view displaying the pleats, 1708, Metropolitan Museum of Art, New York, 1991.6.1a, b.

rectangular shapes. The skirts were extended with gored segments, which create volume at the bottom. There was only a simple curve at the armhole (Waugh, 1968, diagram IX; Arnold, 1989, p. 71). The tops of the pleats were secured to a bodice lining, again primarily cut in a rectangular fashion, which formed a supportive foundation for the pleated silks. This foundational structure of a pleated back mounted onto a fitted lining was fundamental to all gown making until the 1780s: an impressively long lifespan for a construction process.

From the 1740s, the mantua's progeny diverged into the two most recognisable styles of the century: the sack and the English gown. Both styles have been identified, by both contemporaries and scholars of fashion history, by a plethora of names. The sack, which is often called a *robe à la Française*, was generally known in the eighteenth century as a negligee. The English gown, which is often called a *robe à l'Anglaise*, was known as a nightgown. This terminology is often

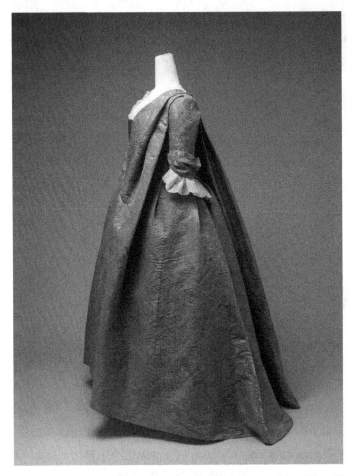

**Figure 4** Robe Volante, 1730, Metropolitan Museum of Art, New York, 2010.148.

paired, with one term providing the contrast to the other: the sack and the English gown (or simply gown), the *robe à la Française* and the *robe à l'Anglaise*, and the negligee and the nightgown. At a 1760s court trial, for example, a mantuamaker was called as a witness for her client and was asked 'would she have a nightgown or a negligee?' (Gurney, 1768, p. 133). In her album recording her fashion consumption over nearly eighty years, Barbara Johnson uses the terms 'gown' and 'nightgown', and 'sack' and 'negligee' interchangeably (Rothstein, 1987; Dyer, 2019a; Dyer, 2021).

In both styles, the fundamentals of the mantua remain. The geometrically cut lengths of fabric continued to be stitched down to a lining that was fitted to the body, but the arrangement of the outer fabric was done in two contrasting ways. In the sack or negligee, the back fabric was arranged in stacked box pleats, which were stitched down only for the first few inches, before falling

**Figure 5** Sack or Negligee, back view, 1760, Los Angeles County Museum of Art, M.56.6a-b.

open into the trailing pleats reminiscent of the volante (Figure 5). The front of the bodice has now been separated from the skirts by a waist seam, although full length robings, reaching from the shoulder straps to the floor were often incorporated (Figure 6). The robings, which consisted of a strip of fabric approximately two inches wide which bordered the front opening of the gown, usually stopped a few inches below the waist. They could be cut along with the front bodice out of a single piece of fabric and folded back on themselves, or applied as a simple strip of fabric after construction was otherwise completed.[14] Later in the century, robings were often omitted entirely. Their purpose was to conceal the many pins with which the gowns were attached to the stays beneath.

---

[14] For an example of applied robings see, for example, National Trust: KIL/W/05266/I.

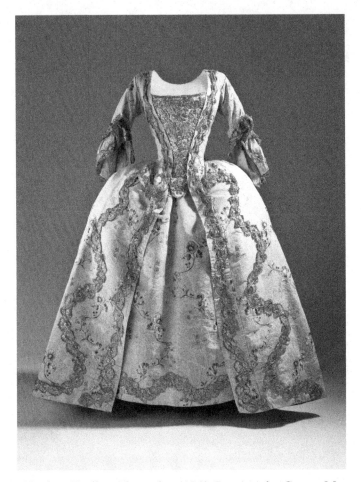

**Figure 6** Sack or Negligee, front view, 1760, Los Angeles County Museum of
Art, M.56.6a-b.

The English gown, or nightgown, was constructed on almost identical lining
shapes. On both styles, the lining was usually draped on the body of the wearer
and fitted directly to the silhouette moulded by their stays.[15] Occasionally,
a pattern would be taken from an existing gown that fitted well if the client
was at a distance, or the maker was working to clothe their own body. In 1763,
Mary Peers, a mantuamaker in Chester, advertised that 'Ladies in the Country
may be fitted with the greatest exactness by sending a Gown as a Pattern'.[16]
While the sack can be identified by its stacked box pleats tumbling down the

---

[15] The decades of experience in draping linings accumulated by the staff at Colonial Williamsburg
has been condensed into a course taught by former employees Christina Johnson and
Brooke Welborn, *To Cut the Perfect Shape: The Fundamentals of Cutting and Fitting to The
Figure* (Burnley and Trowbridge, 2022).

[16] *Adams Weekly Courant*, 5 July 1763.

**Figure 7a** Close-up back view of the pleats of an English gown, 1770–1780, Victoria and Albert Museum, T.104-1972.

**Figure 7b** Full back view of the pleats of an English gown, 1770–1780, Victoria and Albert Museum, T.104-1972.

back of the gown, the English gown is distinguished by its twin sets of pleats, which are clung to the lining beneath, secured by rows of stitching, but cut in one with the skirts beneath (Figures 7a, 7b, and 8). The fronts of English gowns were treated similarly to the sack, with either folded, applied, or no robings

**Figure 8** English gown, back view, 1765–1775, Victoria and Albert Museum, 760-1899.

(Figure 9). It is very difficult to distinguish between the two gowns from the front view alone.

By the 1740s, the columnar shape of the mantua had expanded, first into a bell-like shape, before flattening and protruding only at the hips. From above, the silhouette appeared like an oblong, extending out at the sides, but relatively flat at the back and front. Supported by paniers or hoops, this structure varied both in the width and in the severity of curve from the waist to the widest point of the hip. Some paniers projected at a right angle to waist, creating a dramatic and harsh horizontal line, and were usually worn for the most formal of occasions. Others tapered gradually, creating a more gentle, rounded shape. For general everyday wear, many women wore no paniers at all, and supported their gowns with petticoats, which were sometimes quilted. The shape of the skirt supports often dictated how the gown would be worn. The large court dresses of the mid-century, for example, necessitated a similarly vast hoop skirt. From the 1770s, the emphasis shifted away from the hips and towards the rear, necessitating the concurrent development of skirt supports to match. These supports were often pads known as cork rumps or bums, which exaggerated the back of skirts (Gernerd, 2023, pp. 73–108).

**Figure 9** English gown, front view, 1765–1775, Victoria and Albert Museum, 760-1899.

Sleeves on both styles of gown were very similar, although they fluctuated in style and decoration at the cuff. These variations reflected both shifting modes and trends, as well as the different properties of textiles. Earlier in the century, sleeves were shorter and looser, with the cuff produced by pleating up the end of the sleeve, a small separate cuff mimicking this effect was attached (Arnold et al., 2021, p. 28).[17] Gradually, sleeves tightened around the arm and lengthened to the elbow by the mid-century, before scooping around it and making their way towards the wrist by the turn of the nineteenth century. Early in the century, cuffs could be pleated rectangles of fabric, which imitated the all-in-one look of early mantuas, and extended the geometric cutting techniques. These might be stiffened with paper and contain lead weights to help them maintain their sharp shape (Arnold et al., 2021, p. 33).[18] From the mid-century, these were gradually superseded by tiered flounces, with the curved edges either pinked, if cut from a firm silk, or finished with a minuscule rolled hem.[19]

---

[17] See, for example, Tyne and Wear Archives and Museums: TWCMS: J9805.
[18] See, for example, National Museums Scotland: K.2002.510.
[19] Pinking involves using a sharp stamp to cut the edge of the silk into decorative patterns.

**Figure 10** Italian gown, back view, Metropolitan Museum of Art, New York, 2009.300.647.

From the 1770s, these relatively clear delineations in style were disrupted. As the pace of fashion news increased, the varieties of new gown styles also rapidly diversified. On the English gown, the stomacher disappeared, and the bodice now stretched around the torso to pin closed at the centre front. The most widely adopted addition to the gown family tree was the 'Italian' gown.[20] Instead of stitched down pleats, like the English gown, this style featured a pieced bodice back, cut separately from the skirts and with side-back seams (Figure 10).[21] Although jackets had

---

[20] *The Lady's Magazine* (London, 1780), 143. The use of this terminology is based on informed speculation, as there is no decisive link between the term and the style of gown. The phrase "Italian gown" first appears in newspaper advertisements for stollen gowns in 1778. See, for example, *Public Advertiser,* 10 February 1778, 3. Advertisements for mantuamakers also list it alongside 'sacque' and 'night gowns' for sale in the 1780s. See, for example, *Morning Post,* 20 March 1782, 4.

[21] The pieced back requires cutting separate, shaped pattern pieces for the bodice which match the lining, instead of pleating down a large uncut width of silk to fit the lining beneath.

sometimes been cut this way earlier in the century, this was the first time that a gown included a complete waist seam in over a century.[22] Other new additions to the sartorial assortment and lexicon included the *robe à la piémontaise* and the *robe à la Polonaise*. The former saw the sack pleats separated from the back of the gown. Instead of integral to the construction, they were instead simply draped over the back of an already completed bodice.[23] The *robe à la Polonaise*, also referred to as a 'polonese' or 'poloneze' was cut in four pieces – two backs and two fronts – without a waist seam, and its skirts were looped up with cords (Figure 11).[24] The English gown, meanwhile, was experiencing new subtle

**Figure 11** Polonese gown, back view, Metropolitan Museum of Art, New York, 34.112a, b.

---

[22] Historians of dress in the twentieth century, such as Janet Arnold, misidentified the English gown as '*en fourreau*', resulting in much terminological confusion (Arnold, *Patterns of Fashion 1*, p. 36).

[23] See, for example, Metropolitan Museum of Art: C.I.61.11.

[24] Like the gown '*en fourreau*', the polonese has also been frequently misidentified (Van Cleave and Welborn, 2013).

**Figure 12** English gown, 1775, back view, Los Angeles County Museum of Art, M.70.85.

changes. The back pleats, once two to three inches across the back at the waist, had shrunk down to a single inch, and sometimes turned in to face the centre back seam (Figure 12).[25]

The dawning of the 1790s would see even more radical shifts in both dominant styles and construction methods, as waistlines rose and structures loosened to align with the growing obsession with the classical (Ribeiro, 1995, p. 113; Rauser, 2020). The muslin chemise robe of the 1780s morphed into the high-waisted columnar styles of the regency, and gradually the mechanisms of eighteenth-century mantuamaking fell away as they were replaced by reimaginings of how gowns could function. 1790s gowns often show evidence of inventive initiative being taken to raise waistlines of Italian or English gowns to fit this new sartorial norm (Figure 13). Here, the skirt fabric was either folded up or unstitched and reattached at a new higher waistline level, preserving the earlier construction of the upper part of the bodice. However, by 1800 both the garment construction and the bodily dressing process had radically shifted, and the mantua's dynasty gave way to new and inventive modes of making.[26]

---

[25] Another example of this can be found at National Trust: 1348729.

[26] The layers underneath most eighteenth-century gowns will be discussed in the following section, as part of the dressing process.

**Figure 13** Gown, 1770s, remade in 1790s, Victoria and Albert Museum, IS.3-1948.

## 2.2 Gown Makers: The Hands That Stitched

Chronological histories of fashion's evolution often overlook the hands of the maker. Seamlines move, hemlines rise and fall, and sleeves lengthen and shorten with a sense of assumed and organic inevitability. That human hands had to engineer each change, demonstrating an intimate knowledge of how textiles would behave on the body, is disregarded in favour of an easily digestible narrative of progressive change (Petrov, 2019, pp. 107, 178, 203). By reinserting the hand of the maker into these narratives, the notions of progression and improvement often aligned with chronology give way to more nuanced tales of innovation, experimentation, failure, and inquisitiveness. Hands harnessed textiles, guiding them through the evolutions and deviations in style throughout the mantua's bloodline.

Like the terms applied to garments, the sartorial trades were not as clearly delineated as they might appear. New professions emerged and evolved with designations connected to the shifting fashions. Early in the century, the mantuamaker appeared as the crafter of the mantua, but this transfigured into the dressmaker as the mantua's influence declined. Similarly, body-makers morphed into staymakers as terminology shifted. Yet this synergy between the trades and their related garments was not clear cut. As convenient as it would be to categorise garments as exclusively the realm of specific makers, in practice making was far more fluid. Milliners, who usually traded in accessories and small items, might also make gowns.[27] By 1805, the *Book of Trades*, which was an educational guide for children about the various professions available to them, claimed that the dressmaker made every article of women's dress 'except those which belong to the head and the feet'.[28] Tailors, meanwhile, remained the primary (although not exclusive) makers of riding habits, but later in the century even the *Taylor's Complete Guide* readily renounced habit making, stating that it was 'seldom practiced, and unknown to thousands of Taylors; ... quite dissimilar as joinery and cabinet-making', reflecting a tension between specialisation and plurality of sartorial skill (quoted in Taylor, 2020, p. 154). Shops more broadly were also evolving through the eighteenth century and warehouses, which sold a vast array of sartorial goods, further complicated matters (Walsh, 1995; Stobart et al., 2007; Stobart and Blondé, 2014). Prichard's Warehouse in London described themselves as 'riding habit and robe maker to her majesty', whilst also making stays.[29] The sartorial trades were distinct terminologically, but diverse, interconnected, and overlapping in practice.

This flexibility in terms of which makers made what garments reflects that it is impossible to assume that all gowns – both those that circulated in the eighteenth century and those which survive in museum collections today – were stitched by the hands of makers who identified as mantuamakers. While they likely were responsible for most gowns, many others were stitched by makers in otherwise-titled sartorial trades who had not undertaken a formal apprenticeship or training in a specific process of making. Debates surrounding the turbulent rise of the mantuamaker and their struggles against the tailors' guilds have inadvertently privileged these professional makers over amateur makers (Inder, 2020, pp. 16–20). Similarly, a focus on the business histories of these professional makers, while undoubtedly vital for understanding both the

---

[27] For example, Sabine Winn's London Milliner, Ann Charlton, supplied her with a gown in 1783. See West Yorkshire Archive Service: WYW1352/3/4/6/8, 22 May 1783. See also advertisements for work which claim diverse knowledge, such as 'A Person every Way qualified for a Lady's Woman, would be glad to engage herself in a genteel Family in that Capacity; she understands mantua-making, millinery, and Hair-dressing; and would be glad to live with a lady that travels', *The Public Advertiser*, 12 May 1778.

[28] *The Book of Trades, or, Library of the Useful Arts* (London, 1805), III, 37.

[29] Guildhall Library: Trade cards and billheads for Prichard's Warehouse, 1767, 1770, 1779, 1780 and 1781.

ways in which the trade functioned and women in business, has also unintentionally reinforced an assumption that mantuamakers were responsible for almost all gown making (Birt, 2021). The business records of these makers provide an archival trace of an otherwise tacit, material, embodied, and experiential transaction. The financial exchanges recorded in bills and accounts offer evidence of making at the point of consumption. Yet removed from the commercial world, making is often left unrecorded, or at least inconsistently chronicled.

The troublesome discrimination between the perceived artisanal expertise of the (male) tailor and the procedural and artless toil of the (female) seamstress has also infiltrated scholarship on the mantuamaker. Claudia Kidwell draws a clear delineation between the 'skill' of cutting out and the 'labour' of sewing (1979, p. 3). This hierarchical distinction ranks skill along gendered lines, which aligns with contemporary rhetoric, but has little basis in making practice. Cutting and stitching are distinct but interrelated skills: a cutter must know how a garment is constructed to know where seam allowances are required and how the pieces will interlock, while a sewer must comprehend how to transfigure the flat cut shapes into a three-dimensional garment. Both skills are equally fundamental and transformative in the garment-making process and, as with many skills, the value applied to them is cultural and contextual rather than practically demonstrable. One is not an art while the other mere labour; both are similarly arduous and adroit. In tailoring, cutting into expensive wools and silks was the work of the master tailor, while apprentices stitched the cut pieces together, and perhaps it is this internal tailoring distinction – born of the value of fabric and the perils of expensive mistakes – which has reinforced this divide (Zakim, 2003, p. 130; Ginsburg, 1972). Yet mantuamakers also cut into inordinately expensive fabrics.[30] This peculiar divorcing of skill from women's stitchery seems to be confined to the sartorial trades dominated by women, and extends to cultural perceptions of the two trades. The quintessential image of a tailor – sat cross-legged on the table, engrossed in the dexterous, mysterious, and transformative work of his stitching– is never derided as merely labouring.

In the cultural imagination, the tailor was granted mystical sartorial powers. As Robert Campbell wrote in his much-quoted 1747 *The London Tradesman*, a tailor 'ought to have a quick Eye to steal the Cut of a Sleeve ... Any Bungler may cut out a Shape when he has a Pattern before him but a good Work-man takes it by his Eye in the passing of a Chariot' (1747, p. 192). This innate

---

[30] The cut between the bodice back and the skirts is particularly perilous and, if done incorrectly, can result in the loss of hours of labour as well as expensive materials. See Section 3 for a detailed discussion of this process. Carolyn Dowdell and John Styles have both cited this as a reason why professional cutting was privileged over amateur cutting (Styles, 2007, p. 160; Dowdell, 2021, p. 189).

virtuosity at recognising and translating an observed sartorial feature into a two-dimensional scheme for cutting with alarming alacrity, Campbell states, is the tailor's 'genius'. 'Mr Fashioner', as Campbell styles the instinctively talented tailor, was a 'Shape Merchant[s]' (p. 194). Campbell allows that the mantua-maker also has genius, but hers is as a 'Mistress of the Art of Dissimulation' (p. 227; Batchelor, 2005, p. 55). Her skill at pretence must be primarily directed towards 'a vast Stock of Patience to bear the Tempers of most of the Customers', but her beguiling arts might also lead her into moral peril. While Campbell is able to provide some outline of the practice of almost all the other (male-dominated) trades described in the volume, three quarters of the entry on mantuamakers is devoted to ensuring that young apprentices and journeywoman avoid 'the Snares laid for them by designing Men' because a 'Girl is such a tender, ticklish Plant to rear, that there is no permitting her out of Leading-strings till she is bound to a husband' (p. 228). Dripping in misogyny, Campbell framed the mantuamaker as the 'sister' of the tailor and, like any obedient sibling, she was expected to marry rather than to become threateningly independent.

Despite Campbell's scathing dismissal of the mantuamaker as a skilled and expert maker, formal training within the sartorial trades was widespread. Girls were apprenticed to mantuamakers, and even sometimes tailors, throughout the century (Buck, 1979; Ginsburg, 1972). Mantuamaking apprenticeships were not regulated to the same standard or extent as those for tailors, yet despite this disparate legal and political status, the apprenticeship system nevertheless set up girls as trained and professional makers (Inder, 2020, p. 5). Once they completed their apprenticeships, they might go on to work as journeywomen or, if they had the capital, set up their own establishment. Of course, mantuamaking as a profession required not just proficiency with a needle, but with business, accounting, and commercial operations (Birt, 2021). Coins as well as thread passed through their hands.

This diminishment of the mantuamaker as a skilled and expert maker and businesswoman extended to her domesticated representation in visual culture. In depictions such as Louis Phillipe Boitard's *The Merchant Taylors* (1749) the tailor was generally depicted as an expert at work, and even Thomas Rowlandson's highly satirical *Miseries of Human Life* series sincerely commended 'the complicated profession of a Taylor'.[31] However, the mantuamaker, as well as her sister-maker, the milliner, was often dismissed from the professional world and depicted in quasi-domestic settings.[32] Seated around a table –

---

[31] For Boitard, a print can be found at British Museum: G,12.111; for the preparatory sketch, see Royal Collection's Trust, RCIN 913279. For the Rowlandson, see Lewis Walpole Library: 807.10.00.03.

[32] There was certainly fluidity between mantuamaker's homes and businesses. Often, mantuamakers had private chambers rather than shops. See Gowing (2021).

**Figure 14** Henry Kingsbury, *A Milliner's Shop*, 1787. Courtesy of the Lewis Walpole Library, Yale University.

often analogous with those used for dining or taking tea – women gather, gossip, and stitch. Their skill is reduced to a pastime. Long after the tailoring monopoly was broken at the start of the century, this cultural perception of women's work as a household chore or accomplishment rather than economically productive business endured. Even professional women makers depicted in commercial settings appear as familial huddles, relegated to the corners and away from the main commercial business at hand. In Henry Kingsbury's 1787 *A Milliner's Shop* (Figure 14), the royal family are represented as genteel shoppers. The commercial activity at the shop counter is balanced with the making labour located at a round table by the window. There, two women-milliners and an effeminately presented man-milliner stitch new stock for the shop (Dyer, 2020, p. 112). Their labour is on display, but its presentation is cosy, informal, and casual. It is distinct from the industrious workshop of the tailor. In other depictions of seamstresses at work they are situated within parlours and drawing rooms. In *Beauty and Fashion* (1797), two makers sit at a tripod table (Figure 15). Their hands, frozen in print, are nevertheless active and, as Elisabeth Gernerd has stated, 'centred around the pull of a needle and thread' (2020, p. 210). In such depictions, this

**Figure 15** *Beauty and Fashion*, 1797. Courtesy of the Lewis Walpole Library, Yale University.

haptic and active labour is consistently located within domestic or domestic-like settings.[33] These cosy scenes are snug and subdued, idealised depictions of activities which were viewed as mundane and humdrum, routine and ubiquitous. The mystery and expertise of the tailor is not to be found at the hearthside or beside the tea table.

---

[33] Even later trade manuals depict women garment makers in domestic settings. See, for example, the 'Ladies Dress Maker' in *The Book of Trades* (London, 1804). See Rijksmuseum: RP-P-2009–2594.

This uneven framing of sartorial labour as either professionalised and proficient or homely and mundane cannot be detached from contemporary discus-
sions around women's work more broadly. Gendered divisions between the
woman as homemaker and the man as breadwinner were deepened as industrialisation and capitalism tightened their grip on European society (De Vries, 2008).
There is also an overlap here with domestic industry, cottage industry, and the
proto-industrialisation within these (often textile-related) forms of making within
the home (Morgan, 1999, pp. 28–32). Meanwhile historians of women have
fought to reframe women's domestic labour as productive work (Vickery, 1998;
Baudino and Carré, 2005). That stitching was an amusement and accomplishment, described by Ann Bermingham as part of a 'pantomime of elegant feminine
poses', contributed to this diminishment in value (Bermingham, 2000, p. 183).
Packaged as an accomplishment, sewing was part of a genteel culture of performative leisure, which was inherently at odds with professional notions of
productive industry. Sewing, within this culture of accomplishment, was
a domestic amusement, not a skilled profession.[34]

Temporality is an important concept here, especially in relation to the character-
isation of professional and amateur sewing. Often, curatorial practice has meant
that extant garments with poor quality sewing are categorised as the work of
amateur hands, and those with neat, even, and accurate stitches as professional
(Dyer, 2020). While this might have more credence within twentieth-century
fashion, it holds little relevance to eighteenth-century sewing cultures. For professional eighteenth-century makers, value was held within the textile, not the labour
(Ginsburg, 1972, p. 68; Styles, 2007, p. 160). Speed was, therefore, the priority of
the professional maker. Time was the professional maker's key commodity, and so
sewing was undertaken with temporal efficiency in mind. The more garments
a mantuamaker produced, the more money they would make, and profits were
already slim for the majority of makers. Removed from the commercial world and
undertaken in an amateur capacity, the temporalities of garment making were
reconfigured. In 1781, Louisa Stuart wrote to her sister that 'my chief amusement
since I came from town has been making myself a white polonaise, in which I have
succeeded to a miracle, and repent having given one to a famous mantua maker in
Dublin who spoilt it entirely for me' (1895, p. 169). Stuart's temporal privilege as
an aristocratic woman sewing for herself rather than for a wage may have contributed to this comparative satisfaction with her own work. Taxonomising professional and amateur making based on perceived skill is intensely misleading.
Sartorial expertise is not the pivotal category of difference, but time.

---

[34] For depictions of sewing as a domestic amusement, see, for example, British Museum,
2010,7081.974.

Madeleine Ginsburg unflinchingly referred to eighteenth-century mantua-making as 'thrown-together' and 'slipshod', and disparagingly commented that she had begun to wonder whether the makers had received any training at all (1972, p. 68). The interiors of many extant gowns from the period are certainly loosely constructed; but, as will be elaborated in the subsequent section, this was often for reasons of efficiency and sartorial literacy. Makers knew where the strain would and would not fall on a garment and adjusted their stitching accordingly. Remaking was also a key concern here, as Carolyn Dowdell has demonstrated (Dowdell, 2021; Fennetaux, Junqua and Vasset, 2014). The rob-ings on an English gown from the 1760s might be unfolded, pressed, and transformed into a closed fronted iteration of the gown, popular in the 1770s. This alteration process also explains why the separate shoulder strip appeared on this later form of gown – an innovation which is otherwise unnecessary.[35] Eighteenth-century hands could stitch with incredible accuracy, as is to be found in contemporary shifts, shirts, and other frequently laundered linens, but they also stitched with proportionate and appropriate efficiency.

Sources depicting women as professional garment makers are limited, and rarely do we see inside the mantuamakers workroom in the way we have access to the tailor's shop. Denis Diderot's 1751 *Encyclopedie* offers a rare view into the workings of a French *Couturiere* (Figure 16) (Sheridan, 2009). Although the French and British gown-making trades operated differently, the limited array of sources mean that this representation has held considerable influence in informing how mantuamakers and milliners working lives are understood (Haru Crowston, 2001; Chrisman-Campbell, 2015). The working recreation of Margaret Hunter's millinery shop in Colonial Williamsburg, for example, is heavily influenced by the image (Cabell, 1988). Similarly, François Alexandre Pierre de Garsault's 1769 *L'Art du Tailleur* offered a second insight into the workings of the French sartorial trades, although elements are almost exactly copied from Diderot (1763, pl. 15). This pair of texts have shaped much of the existing literature on mantua-making, both within and beyond France. In so doing, a universalised system of making has been assumed, which allows little space for the heterogeneity and variation that is reflected in extant garments. The hands of individual makers are blurred together within these formalised compendiums of making.

Key mantuamaking skills have been usefully gleaned from Diderot and Garsault, most notably surrounding the relationship between makers, making, and the body. The processes usefully deducted from these images and their accompanying text are those surrounding measuring and fitting. The measuring

---

[35] Its additional purpose is to enclose the top raw edge of the sleeve head, but other solutions to this issue were available.

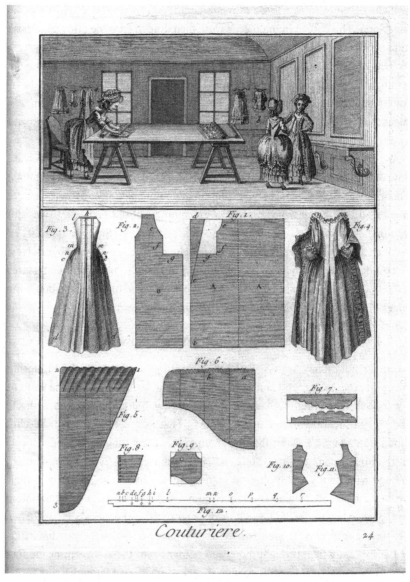

**Figure 16** Denis Diderot, *Couturiere*, 1751. Author's own collection.

process was conducted by cutting sixteen notches into a long strip of paper, each notch corresponding with a different measure on the client's body. No numerical measurements were taken. These notched measures were used to determine the dimensions of the geometric shapes which formed the bulk of the gown. Inches were only used when they supplemented the notched measures, for example Garsault directs that pieces should be cut 'several inches' longer than the measure taken by the maker, to allow for hemming (1769, p. 49). Even here, an inch is employed as a loose measurement rather than to ascertain a precise dimension. The bodice lining pieces were then draped onto the body, and these geometric pieces built onto those linings.[36] Unlike tailors, who worked with patterns and drafted their cutting lines on the flat surface of a large table, the mantuamaker's primary workspace was their client's bodies. Without the dictation of patterned shapes and uniform modes of curved cuts, mantuamaking was intensely focused on the client's body. Clothes were made to wrap around and encase the body, whatever irregularities it might possess.

As Amanda Vickery has observed, economic shifts in women's labour are slow and messy (1993). The capitalist and gendered structures of professional labour, whilst fundamental to the evolution of mantuamaking as a trade, obscure the skill of the hands whose labour was commercialised. That skill was not recorded in instruction manuals or records of training (Smith et al., 2017). Instead, it is imbued within the fruits of that labour: the gowns themselves. The products of those busy hands sit encased in Tyvek tombs in museum stores and, although they cannot be read with the convenience of the recipe book, the traces of their makers' labour endure in their stitches and folds.

## 3 Recreating the English Gown

Garments hold many secrets. From the ubiquitous sweat stains found lurking under sleeves, to the food and drink splatters which trickled down the front of a waistcoat belonging to George III in his frailty, human interaction with the material garment permeates such objects.[37] These signs of wear resonate with Linda Baumgarten's claim that the 'human spirit has long connected with its past' through such objects (2002, p. 204). Such clothes were worn, dirtied, imbued with bodily and biological matter. Human lives reside lurking in their weaves and seams. Studies of wear, mending, and reuse are vital in reanimating limp garments with the bodies which once wore them (Fennetaux et al., 2014). Yet such studies elevate the wear and maintenance of garments over the hands of the makers which brought them into being. From the silkworm or the flax seed to the consumer's wardrobe, the garment transitioned through many forms and passed through the hands of many makers (Anishanslin, 2016). Garments hold not just the stories of their wearers, but also of their makers.

The object – or rather the garment – as a central focus within studies of dress and textiles is widespread within the field. David Jules Prown's approach to the study of material culture has been expressly adapted for dress history by Ingrid Mida and Alexandra Kim, who translate Prown's 'description, deduction, and

---

[36] This process will be elaborated on in relation to the recreation in the next section.
[37] Historic Royal Palaces: HRP2624364.

speculation' into 'observation, reflection, and interpretation' (Prown, 1982; Mida and Kim, 2018; Ribeiro, 1998; Riello, 2013). Materially attentive approaches to dress history, which align the object with textual and visual evidence, are dominant in the field (for example, Burman and Fennetaux, 2019). Mida, in particular, is a proponent of close looking through drawing.[38] This method enacts a close visual intimacy with the garment, forcing the researcher to question assumptions and to look deeply into the components and composition of a garment. Recreation, I suggest, takes this even further. Instead of looking at where a seam holds a particular garment together, it allows the researcher to question how and why the maker decided to place and work a seam in a particular way. Procedural questions, like how a hem was worked or the order of construction, can be answered, as well as deeper enquiries into the cultural dimensions of sartorial labour. That tacit, embodied experience of the maker springs forth through recreation, connecting making hands across the centuries.

A fundamental aspect of Michael Polanyi's writings on the tacit is that 'we can know more than we can tell' (Polanyi, 1966, p. 4). Within recreative practice, this presents a thorny methodological and interpretive consideration. Acting as both researcher and research subject, the recreative practitioner may uncover more knowledge, experience, and understanding than it is possible to translate into written forms. The very problem that recreative researchers aim to solve – how the making of the past can be translated from its tacit state – perpetuates in that process of conversion from experiential affect to comprehensible prose. The knowledge generated through recreative practice is intensely personal and always partial. As Richard Sennet has suggested, demonstration is a vital form of training, but it is often lost in text (Sennett, 2009, p. 181). To present such tacit knowledge in a lucid way which a non-maker might understand poses unique challenges. Woodyard's approach to this issue was an auto-ethnographical process of filming, research diary, and interviews with a colleague (2017, pp. 27–32). This method has been adapted here, focusing on the filming of the process, alongside reflective writings authored at intervals during the sewing process. This capture of the making process may then be critically examined, taking into account both the bodily movements captured on film and the maker's musings and observations.

This approach, as Nithikul Nimkulrat has observed, offers a way of 'thinking through the hand manipulating a material' via 'logically thinking through the senses' (2021, p. 1; 2010, p. 77). The hand, in this process, becomes a site of cognition, feeding back and enacting its labour upon the fabric. Writing as a creative practitioner, Nimkulrat goes on to argue that the 'craftwork of an artist is not

---

[38] University College London's '100 hours' project similarly promoted intense close looking as fundamental to material culture studies (Smith and Hannan, 2017).

secondary to thinking or the intuition of the artist, and they are not separated acts' (2010, p. 77). Body and mind are so frequently divorced within Western philosophy, which detaches 'mental, intellectual, and emotional capacities' (Pallasmaa, 2009, p. 12). Recreation, and an autoethnographic approach to its interpretation, work to reforge the (conceptually) severed links between cognition and the body. Knowledge and skill reside in the hands and body, as well as the mind. Repeated processes, such as the easy rhythm of a needle pushed in and out of the fabric to form a running stitch, are enacted instinctively. The hands hold the knowledge.

This embodied knowledge is fundamental to accessing the practices, skills, and cultures of eighteenth-century garment making. Yet scholars have been all too ready to diminish the skill of the mantuamaker, perpetuating the gendered division of skill found in contemporary rhetoric (Ginsburg, 1972; Kidwell, 1979). At a workshop held at the University of Warwick in 2017, the event broke out from traditional academic papers and into making workshops.[39] There, researchers whose usual tool was the pen were instead encouraged to pick up their own needles. When the implements of the craft they write about were thrust into their hands, the narrative changed. When they were cast as the maker, sewing was too complicated, they did not know how to do it. Just as modern art is sometimes divisively derided as something a child could do, it is all too easy to dismiss the skills of a maker when one has not attempted to make themselves (Hodge, 2012). There is no intellectual objectivity gained through observing rather than doing. Without active and participatory knowledge of making, knowledge is truncated, limited, and abridged.

Within this project, the making hand is turned towards the English gown, variably also known as the nightgown or *robe a l'Anglaise*. Within the mantua's family tree of gowns which dominated the century, this was perhaps the most ubiquitous, occupying a space in wardrobes across the social spectrum, from royalty to some working women. In various forms, it was also the most tenacious style of gown, outlasting the sack gown into the 1780s. The recreation process was conducted in three stages, following the tripartite structure modelled by Prown, Mida, and Kim. The method commenced with an (i) *object-based analysis* of extant examples held in museum collections. Then, those objects were (ii) *decoded* into a comprehensible method and order of making. Finally, the (iii) *enactment and interpretation* of this making process was captured via a dual film and reflective writing method (Heath et al., 2010).

---

[39] *Fashioning Dress: Sewing and Skill, 1500-1850*, conference and historical sewing skills workshop, University of Warwick, 19 May 2017. Similar events that incorporated making into a conference include *Uncovering Material Knowledge*, Queens University Belfast, 30–31 August 2019; *Unpacking the V&A Wedgwood Collection*, Victoria and Albert Museum, 7 July 2023.

## 3.1 Decoding Sartorial Methods

Recreative methods must be embedded within material culture studies (Harvey, 2009; Riello, 2012; Gerritsen and Riello, 2015; Dyer, 2021). While some projects are rooted in recipes and instructions, an awareness of the material evidence – however sparse it may be – remains imperative. Even within medieval and early modern studies, where inventories and scraps of descriptive text outnumber surviving garments, those garments continue to be crucial (Mikhaila and Malcolm-Davies, 2006; Malcolm Davies, Johnson and Mikhaila, 2008; Payne et al., 2011). Within this project, it is the scars of seamlines and unravelling stitches which offer the most fertile evidence. The first two stages of the research method outlined earlier will be discussed together here, uniting the object-based analysis undertaken in museum collections with the processes of deduction and decoding necessary to rebuild a method of making.

Making knowledge is fragmented. The gowns that exist in museum collections have been subject to the influences of many hands, as well as other environmental factors, since they were first made. Alterations and injury – intentional, accidental, and environmental – have occurred many times over since the first pair of hands transformed fabric into garment. The gowns which have endured often wear their battle scars from the fight to survive through the centuries. They may have been compelled to endure the indignities of the dressing up box, the pageantry of the Victorian masquerades, or abandonment in damp attics, before finally finding care and repose in the cool, dark recesses of the museum store.[40] Within such garments, the handiwork of the original maker has been eroded by subsequent remaking, adjustment, and wear, leaving only a trace of some part of the making process. Sometimes, it is straightforward to identify these layers of remaking, as Victorians added poppers or used jarring brightly coloured threads, making no secret of their sartorial anachronisms. Sometimes, the cacophony is too enmeshed, and an intimate knowledge of thread and stitch is required to decipher each layer of making (Sykas, 2000). Recreation presents an opportunity to gather the enduring elements from the original making process which persevere across a range of garments, and to reconstitute them into a comprehensible making process. Adding another 're-' term to the already bulging array of potential terminology (remaking, recreation, reconstruction, replication, reproduction) may appear unhelpful, but in this context, it seems to appropriately reflect a method of building up again from parts. The reconstitution is a stage within a broader process of recreation.

---

[40] This is especially true of the garments from the Snowshill collection, which was originally collected by Charles Paget Wade. Wade held costumed masquerades and pageants throughout his lifetime, using the garments now in the collection (Howard, 2016).

It is important to distinguish historical practices of remaking from scholarly methodologies of recreation. Cultures of remaking were widespread throughout the eighteenth and nineteenth centuries. Once one style of gown fell out of fashion, its fabric was given new life and the gown regenerated to fall in step with the latest styles.[41] By the 1830s and 1840s, to dress in a *robe a la Grand-Mere*, articulated this self-conscious practice of anachronistic and historically aware dressing.[42] Occasionally, this process of remaking was started, but abandoned, the gown left languishing in a fragmented state. One example in the collections of the National Trust shows the shoulder seams unpicked and the sleeves removed, and the linings partially detached from the outer silk, but then the disassembly was apparently abandoned, and the gown remains in this half-deconstructed state (Figure 17). Unpicked garments are surprisingly common and allow unprecedented access to the inner workings of construction. All that is concealed between the outer textile and the lining is revealed through these deconstructed garments. Perhaps even more significantly, such gowns reveal the shapes of each portion of the garment as it was originally cut. Taking patterns from three-dimensional garments is achievable, but always liable to miscalculation. Deflated from their wearable state and collapsed back to a two-dimensional textile, those pattern shapes become apparent. An example of an English gown in the collection of Colonial Williamsburg is especially helpful.[43] Divided up the centre back line, one half remains intact, while the other half has been fully unpicked into its contingent parts. Here, shapes for the bodice front, back lining, and sleeve are revealed, as well as a long gore.[44] The back of the outer gown textile is particularly illuminating, as it displays both the scar lines for the pleats down the back of bodice, as well as the curved cut at the waist which allowed the skirt to be closely pleated up against the bodice.

A total of thirty-eight gowns were studied specifically for this project, building upon over nearly two decades of familiarity with hundreds of such objects in museum collections, as both a researcher and a curator.[45] Of those thirty-eight, five were selected for intimate study. This included two gowns in

---

[41] There are innumerable examples of this, such as Colonial Williamsburg: 1960-713,A. Sometimes gowns were never completed, such as Colonial Williamsburg: 1953-1003,1.

[42] Ruby Hodgson, "Robe a la Grand-Mere: Re-use of 18th-century silk in Romantic era dress" (paper presented at the *Sartorial Society Series*, 29 July 2021). For evidence of this refashioning, see, for example National Trust: NT 1362160.1. This gown was made in the 1840s using a textile from the 1773. See also the Museum at FIT, New York: P87.20.7.

[43] Colonial Williamsburg: 2019-61,A-O.

[44] A gore is a triangular insertion use to increase fullness at the hem without adding bulk to the waist.

[45] These garments are in the collections of the Killerton House, National Trust; Snowshill Manor, National Trust; Leeds Museums and Galleries; Fashion Museum, Bath; Royal Albert Memorial Museum, Exeter; Victoria and Albert Museum; Museum of London; Historic Royal Palaces; and several private collections.

**Figure 17** Partially disassembled sack gown, 1765–1769. National Trust, NT 1350856.

the National Trust's Snowshill Collection (NT 1348707 and NT 1348713.1), two gowns in the collection of Leeds Museums and Galleries (LEEAG 2012.177.3 and LEEAG 2012.177.1), and one gown from the National Trust's Killerton House collection (NT 1360761). These gowns were chosen because they either showcased making methods found present in many gowns from the broader sample, or they exhibited key features or points of divergence in English gown making. Although provenances are loose, this selection also represents a geographical spread across England. As part of the object-analysis process, each of these garments was closely examined, photographed, and patterns, notes, and drawings were taken.[46]

The yellow English gown from the Snowshill Collection is well known amongst historians of dress in this period (Figure 18).[47] It was included in

---

[46] These patterns were not taken with the intension of replicating these extant gowns, but rather to enable comparative assessment of cut and construction.

[47] National Trust: NT 1348707. This gown was also known under the accession number SNO7.

**Figure 18** English gown, 1750s–1760s. National Trust, NT 1348707.

Nancy Bradfield's extensive catalogue of drawings of garments in the Snowshill Collection and was on loan to display in the Victoria and Albert Museum for many years (Bradfield, 1968, pp. 33–34). The gown was made from a mustard yellow wool and lined with densely woven white linen. Although the curatorial notes conjecture that the gown may not have been worn, the evidence on the gown contradicts this claim. Beneath each armpit, stains from perspiration are clearly visible, the tide marks of each layer of sweat layered up like ripples, recording within the fabric of the gown each occasion when it was worn. The robings were cut in one piece with the front bodice panel and folded back to create the front boarder. The back reveals the curved lines of the back pleats, secured in place with spaced back stitches. The sleeves are finished with a double layer falling cuff, and the cuffs as well as the neckline, are trimmed with pleated boarders of the same yellow wool, finished at the edge with a pinking iron.[48] The gown was accompanied by two matching stomachers, both made of the same wool, with the pinked trim applied in differing designs on each. The hands which made this gown produced stitches which were precise and neat. They are impressively even, and meticulously stitched; there is nothing 'slipshod' about this construction (Ginsburg, 1972, p. 68). There is some piecing around the top of the skirt, where lengths of fabric have required seaming together into a longer length. This usually occurs when a maker is trying to make the most of a small supply of fabric, but here it has been undertaken so neatly that it is impossible to see the seam until the gown is examined closely. Economy, durability, and neatness were prioritised in this garment.

Sitting alongside the yellow wool gown in the Snowshill store is another yellow English gown (Bradfield, 1968, pp. 31–32). This example was made from a watered silk, which is surprisingly heavy and crisp. The bodice lining was made from two different qualities of linen and shows the signs of some intriguing fitting issues (Figure 19). Slivers of fabric were added in at the centre

**Figure 19** Diagram of the pieced lining of an English gown showing piecing. Each line represents a stitch line between different pieces of linen stitched together to create the back panel of the lining. 1760s. National Trust, NT 1348713.1.

---

[48] Pinking irons were metal stamps which cut a patterned shape into the edge of the fabric. This prevented fraying and left a decorative boarder. Usually, this boarder was scalloped.

back seam, and under the arm at the side seam, enlarging both the general circumference of the gown, and adding additional width at the bust line. It appears that these additions took place as part of the initial fitting process, as there is no scarring or signs of alteration to the outer silk at these points. It is only possible to conjecture as to why these additions needed to be made, when usual practice was to drape the lining pieces upon the body.[49] Perhaps the gown recycled the lining from a previous gown, or it might be that a pattern was taken from a previous gown, and then alterations were required to adapt it to the clients changing figure. One Norfolk mantuamaker, when unpicking a gown for this purpose in 1797, was astonished to discover £195 of bank notes secreted under the lining.[50] The gown's skirts are also lined in a fine, lightweight ivory silk, which is unusual amongst the gowns studied. The robings, cut in one with the bodice like the previous gown, are on this occasion pleated double, meaning there is an extra decorative pleat along the inner edge of the robing.

A third yellow gown, this time in the collection at Leeds Museums and Galleries, was made from a wool and silk mix (Figure 20).[51] Like the first gown, this is generally very evenly and neatly stitched in a mixture of a heavy yellow silk and undyed linen thread. The selvedge of the fabric (derived from 'self-finished', meaning the clean edge of the fabric created through the weaving process which will not fray) has been put to good use at the centre front opening of the skits and along the neck binding, minimising the need for hems and maximising the use of the fabric. It is lined in a twill woven linen. From the inside, the division of the pleats around the waistline is remarkably uneven, but this is not apparent from the outside and would not show when worn. Perhaps the most intriguing feature is the sleeves. It is usual to see three to six pleats at the sleeve head, used to ease the fabric into the armscye. However, here there are approximately ten pleats, and evidence of attempts to set and then reset the sleeves. The gown presents an intriguing coalescence of skilled and neat craftsmanship with rushed and efficient handling of the fabric. It is the cuffs which are the most impressive. Where they meet the sleeve of the gown, the cuff is first gathered in to match the sleeve's circumference. Several inches up the sleeve, the cuff is then box pleated down. This is a relatively simple method of application, requiring knowledge of basic fabric manipulation but not of any particularly tricky stitches.

The yellow wool and silk gown was acquired by the museum along with other items belonging to the Priestman family, including another English gown in blue and pink striped silk with brocaded flowers.[52] From Thornton-le-Dale near Pickering in Yorkshire, this family were influential Quakers in the area

---

[49] *Book of Trades*, III, 31.    [50] *Norfolk Chronicle*, March 1797.
[51] Leeds Museums and Galleries: LEEAG 2012.177.3.
[52] Leeds Museums and Galleries: LEEAG 2012.177.1.

**Figure 20** Yellow silk and wool gown, 1760s. Leeds Museums and Galleries, LEEAG 2012.177.3.

(Priestman, 1935). John Priestman married Barbara Proctor on 15 June 1763, so it seems likely that these gowns both belonged to her.[53] This intriguing Quaker provenance is perhaps most evident in this second gown, which amalgamates the construction methods and open stomacher front of the 1760s with the closed and curved cuff treatments unique to the 1770s. The textile, with its delicate brocaded design, also appears to be from the 1770s. The construction method is otherwise remarkably similar to its yellow sibling, even down to unusual details like ties across the centre front of the gown to hold it closed,

---

[53] Curator Vanessa Jones has researched this family and their connection to the gowns. Vanessa Jones, "The clothing of Barbara Priestman: Redefining eighteenth-century sartorial narratives within the museum" (paper presented at *Stitches that Speak*, De Montfort University, 20 April 2023.

which are uncommon this late in the century. The shapes and dimensions of the lining pieces are also close to identical in both dresses, but with a slight increase to the waist measurement on the later gown. To speculate, this may indicate that the gowns were made at home, the later gown made following the pattern of the bodice shapes used in the earlier yellow gown.

The final gown which was intimately examined was from the National Trust collection held at Killerton House.[54] From the outside, the gown appears rather sombre and proper. It is made from a dark brown brocade, probably woven early in the century, and appears smart and neat. The spaced back stitches which fasten down the back pleats are tidy, even, and uniform in appearance. But upon pealing open the bodice to reveal the inner workings of the gown, the artifice is exposed. Running stitches, sometimes over an inch long and sewn in a cumbersome thick dark thread, seem to haphazardly travel across the lining of the gown. Jagged stitches catch the sleeves in place, and the ends of threads have been roughly tied off and left to dangle. While the previous gowns were generally constructed with neatness and precision, this gown offers a closer articulation of Ginsburg's interpretation of these gowns as 'thrown-together' (1972, p. 68). From the inside, a cursory glance might fill a modern sewer – used to the elegance of the seam finishes provided by overlockers and French seams – with horror. And yet, as perilous as the interior of the garment may look, it has survived. It has outlived its maker by centuries, endured numerous wears and uses, and it remains unscathed. Its construction may appear deceitful, tricking an onlooker into thinking the gown is perfectly sewn, when the interior is a rough and ready clutter of stitches. Yet this gown speaks to the efficiency of the eighteenth-century hand. More than any other gown examined, it is this one which voices the priorities and pressures incumbent on the hand of the profes-sional mantuamaker. That incongruence between the exterior fastidiousness and interior imprecision is the result of carefully targeted labour by a hand under time pressure. This is not a botched job, laziness, or an unskilled hand at work. These stitches are full of intentionality: there is expert stitching where it matters, and efficient economy where it does not. The application of the sewing hand is allocated according to efficacy and productivity.

The knowledge built up from these gowns was also supplemented by the research of the numerous other makers who have similarly sought to recapture eighteenth-century making knowledge. Perhaps most influential is the immense making knowledge built up within the Margaret Hunter millinery shop at Colonial Williamsburg. Under the direction of Janea Whitacre, the apprentice-ship and internship programmes that this institution runs have guided the hands

---

[54] National Trust: NT 1360761.

of many active recreative practitioners, including Woodyard, Samantha Bullat, Abby Cox, Christina Johnson, and Brooke Welborn, who continue to be active researchers in this area. Johnson and Welborn, and occasionally Bullat, share their knowledge through sewing workshops, Woodyard runs classes and Cox has authored a practical guide on eighteenth-century garment making (Cox and Stowell, 2017).[55] Beyond Colonial Williamsburg, the School of Historical Dress in London, under principal Jenny Tiramani, researches and teaches historical construction methods and publishes new editions of Janet Arnold's *Patterns of Fashion* book series, while independent researchers like Michelle Barker and Dowdell have also sought to understand how garments in this period were constructed by returning to extant examples (Arnold et al., 2021; Barker, 2021; Dowdell, 2010).

Recreative practice knowledge is based on experience, trial, and error, as well as object-based study. It would be disingenuous to present the deductions that follow as the product of a neatly constrained research project. The knowledge behind this project is the product of extensive making undertaken over decades. As Davidson has argued, it is important that recreative practitioners state their background knowledge and skill when approaching a project.[56] Although my own training is as a historian rather than a sewer, I have been experimenting with recreations for two decades, and I have honed my skills and knowledge through multiple trials. Repetition generates expertise, and I approach this project with extensive practical expertise, which I do not pretend to assume is accessible to every researcher. This would not, I hope, deter scholarly hands from beginning their own journey as makers, whatever skills and materials they have at hand.

The information gathered from both my own analysis of extant garments, my experience as a maker, and the research undertaken both within and beyond the academy by Barker, Cox, Dowdell, Johnson, Morrison, Tiramani, Welborn, and Woodyard, has enabled me to reconstitute a representative method of making an English gown. Dowdell has drawn a clear and deliberate distinction between 'sewing techniques' and 'construction methods', which will be followed in this study (Dowdell, 2010, p. 190). The former made up a skillset, possessed by many professional and amateur makers alike, both within and beyond mantua-making. These skills were selected from the sewer's lexicon of stitches, and then enacted and practiced on a particular making project. If stitches were the

---

[55] Bullat, Johnson, and Welborn have designed and delivered workshops for Burnley and Trowbridge; Woodyard runs a handsewing company, Sewn Company.

[56] Davidson made this argument in her keynote, 'Expanding the Embodied Turn: Issues and Directions in Remaking', given at *Replicas, Reconstructions, and Recreations: Defining Terms of Historical Making*, 2nd September 2023, De Montfort University, Leicester, UK.

language, then the gown was the text. Construction methods are distinct, in that they refer to the order of making and the process of assemblage. This might retain shared characteristics across different gowns, but is also a space for variation, experimentation, and idiosyncrasy. These construction methods were not tediously and uniformly repeated. Although based on the same basic principles, in practice, they could be delightfully quirky.

The vocabulary of the sewing hand is its stitches (Video 1). For this project, these included basic stitches still recognisable today, such as the (i) *running stitch*, where the hand works the needle up and down through the fabric in a continuous flow, as well as the (ii) *backstitch*, which is a particularly strong stitch worked back upon itself, and which cannot be pulled out or unravelled like the running stitch. Other stitches include the (iii) *spaced back stitch*, where the thread follows the same path as the backstitch, but a gap is left between each short stitch on the upper side, as well as the (iv) *felling stitch*, which is used in areas like the lining. It is a combination of these basic stitches which are brought together to stitch specialist seams, like the eponymous mantuamakers seam.

Although the order of making and construction methods can be deduced from extant garments, one area of contention amongst practitioners of eighteenth-century garment making surrounds how the initial patterns for the linings were taken. The garments themselves offer very few clues around how this initial component of the gown was shaped. It is these linings upon which the rest of the gown is built, so precision and accuracy in this foundational element are vital. The Colonial Williamsburg method, informed by a handful of contemporary

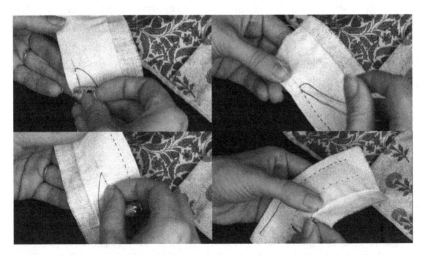

**Video 1** A demonstration of the main hand stitches, author's own footage.

depictions and descriptions, is to drape upon the body.[57] In contrast, Barker uses a flat pattern drafting method more aligned with contemporary tailoring, using the sixteen measures suggested by Diderot.[58] Meanwhile, Morrison has experimented with the various methods available, asking groups of costume-making students to try out the different methods.[59] In practice, it seems likely that there was not one single method. Like the placement of stitching, different makers had different drafting preferences. The Duchess of Montmorency 'employed herself in taking patterns' from gowns belonging to Melesina Trench, before making them up for herself 'with the ingenuity of a milliner or mantuamaker' (1862, p. 330). Yet volumes depicting the trades clearly describe how a maker would take 'the pattern off from a lady by means of a piece of paper or cloth. The pattern, if taken in cloth, becomes afterwards the lining of the dress'.[60] Old dresses, as may have been the case with the yellow watered silk gown, could also be used as the basis for new ones. In 1763, Chester mantuamaker Mary Peers advertised that 'Ladies in the Country may be fitted with the greatest exactness by Sending a Gown as a Pattern'.[61] Without existing pattern shapes to work from, the pattern for this recreation was draped upon the body, using the linen which would become the lining. It was with this initial activity that the enactment and interpretation stages of the recreation commenced.

## 3.2 Reflections on the Making Process

Gown making was a creative and individual process. Nevertheless, it appears to have loosely followed a comparable order of making throughout the extant gowns examined here. The making of the gown occurred in five stages. Firstly, the linings were draped and cut to fit the client's body. Next the back portions of the gown were cut, pleated, and sewn; this process was then repeated with the front sections of the bodice. The skirts were then pleated and attached, and the sleeves made up and inserted. Finally, additional elements like trims and a matching petticoat were made, although these elements have not been included in the core experiment carried out here. To avoid confusion, 'client' will be used to refer to the person the gown is being made to fit, and 'maker' will be used to refer to the person undertaking the draping, fitting, and stitching; although it is acknowledged that not all gowns were made in this bipartite way, and that in some cases, the maker was also the client/wearer (Dyer, 2020). The reflections which follow

---

[57] Johnson and Welborn, *To Cut the Perfect Shape*.

[58] Michelle Barker, *Cut & Construction of a 1730s Mantua* (online course, The Georgian Costume Study Centre, 2022).

[59] Rebecca Morrison, "(Re)making Mantuas: From Seamstresses to Mantua-Makers" (paper presented at the Sartorial Society Series, 10 December 2020).

[60] *The Book of Trades* (London, 1818), 225.     [61] *Adams Weekly Courant*, 5 July 1763.

incorporate a summary of the key actions performed by my hands as a maker, interspersed with relevant sections from the reflective writing undertaken during the making process. This is not intended as a series of instructions or a method for other makers to follow, but rather as a framework for the reflective and critical analysis of the making as an experimental and experiential process. Within this experiment, I acted as both researcher and research subject. This process follows auto-ethnographic principles and methods, adapting them to recreative practice (Chang, 2016; Woodyard, 2017).

### *3.2.1 Draping the Pattern*

This opening act in the process of making requires the sewer to use not stitches, but pins. The maker must first pin three rectangles of linen upon the client's body, which is dressed in the shift, stays, panniers, or hoops, and underpetticoat which will support the silhouette of the gown (Video 2). The bulk of the gown-making process can be achieved with a single pair of hands, but taking pattern shapes from the body is almost impossible without assistance. The client's body must remain upright and straight to ensure a good fit, and twisting and contorting the body to move pins immediately warps the linen. The maker must pin the rectangles of linen together along the desired seam lines, and then gradually smooth and snip the fabric into place. As the gown was made to fit my own body, I was the client in this portion of the experiment:

> It is a strangely intimate experience. My body is under scrutiny. I stay as still as possible and become peculiarly aware of my posture. My hands are motionless, but I remain engaged in the making process. Through the many layers of linen which make up my stays, I can feel the maker's hands pinching and smoothing the linen lining into place. The positioning of the seam lines becomes familiar, as I sense the repeated movement of the maker's hands along those key areas.[62]

The client and maker have a collaborative relationship in this moment. The client's body is not an inanimate mannequin, but responsive and present. This extends to both the sensation of the maker's hands moving over the client's body and the communication between maker and client, as the latter indicated their preference for how they wish various features of the gown to fall. The body of the client must also move when commanded. Arms must be raised to allow for the armscye (the curved area where the sleeve will fit) to be marked, and movements must be undertaken to make sure there is range of motion. Further measures are also taken, such as the distance between the waist and the floor, accounting for the bulk created by the underpinnings.

---

[62] *Reflective Diary*, 19 January 2023.

**Video 2** The undergarments worn beneath the gown and during the fitting process, author's own footage. Video file available at www.cambridge.org/Dyer

Once refined and marked out, the maker must unpin the linen lining/pattern pieces from the client's body and lay them flat on the worktable. At this stage, the maker may neaten curves and sharpen the straight lines. However, if the maker observes variations caused by irregularities on the client's body, such as discrepancies in bust size between the left and right side, they must be left unaltered. The maker then cats away all the excess fabric, leaving only a small amount for seam allowances. The fundamental shapes – the back, front, and sleeve (Figure 21) – are the features which dictate fit, and the client's body is now released until it is recalled for fittings later in the process.

### 3.2.2 Constructing the Backs

The sewer now begins stitching in earnest. The backstitch, the most robust and secure of all the stitches, is used sparingly in the construction process. When removed, backstitches leave the most scaring in the precious textiles, and so are to

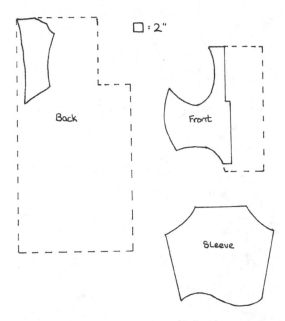

**Figure 21** A scale diagram of the patterns taking from the draping process, overlaid with the cutting diagram for the outer textile, author's own image.

be avoided. Where it is used, it is placed deliberately where the gown will experience the most strain when worn. One of these areas is the centre back seam. This was stitched with a linen thread, which is coated in beeswax prior to stitching to help the thread pass smoothly through the fabric.[63] Where it was possible to access this stitching on extant gowns, the number of backstitches to the inch in this region varied, but eight to ten stitches per inch would provide a solid seam. The backstitch presented a moment of intensity: 'my hand movements are small, then large as I pull the thread away, creating a rhythmic flow of movement with metronomic regularity'.[64] Once stitched, this piece (or its paper facsimile) was used to mark the corresponding centre back seamline in the outer textile. The outer textile, in this case a silk taffeta, was folded in half width wise, and the back shape placed near the fold (Video 3). It is the placement of this line which dictates how the centre back pleats are angled and fall:

> Aligning the centre back piece required a practiced eye and an awareness of grainline. Mental agility was required to plan the impact that these decisions,

---

[63] And 80/2 linen thread was used, which is a strong but fine weight of thread. The first number indicates the thickness of the thread, while the second number relates to number of strands, also known as the ply of a thread. The needles used were sharps #10.

[64] *Reflective Diary*, 30 January 2023.

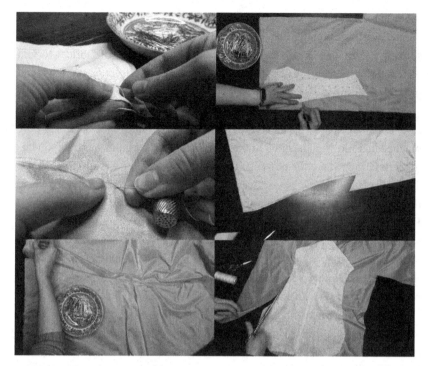

**Video 3** The process of cutting and stitching the back panel of the gown, author's own footage. Video file available at www.cambridge.org/Dyer

made early in the process, would have upon later outcomes. This presented a kind of pressure, but also a sense of synergy between mind and hand. The aesthetic of the final gown lies with this single placement.[65]

One of the significant points of fashionable change between the 1740s and 1780s was the width and angle of the pleats on the back of the English gown, and it is in these early moments of construction that the characteristics of this feature are decided. Once satisfied with the position of the centre back seam on the silk, the sewer marks and stitches this line, again in a backstitch, but this time it is worked in a silk thread. The measures taken during the fitting are then used to inform where excess silk may be cut away, which will be used later for cutting out smaller portions of the gown, like the neck bindings, ruffled cuffs, and trim.

Any remaining excess fabric is then trimmed away by the sewer, the seam opened, and aligned with the lining piece. An iron was unnecessary, as the seams could be finger pressed open, meaning the seam allowance was pushed

---

[65] *Reflective Diary*, 30 January 2023.

back and the folds of the seam compressed between the fingers; the body's natural warmth moulded the fabric beneath. The sewer then uses a basting stitch – a long loose stitch for temporarily attached pieces of fabric – to join the centre back seam, which presented 'an opportunity to relax the wrist and proceed with speed'.[66]

The sewer may now put the needle aside, and the maker's hands switch their style of labour again. Two pleats are taken down each side of the back. They are pinched in, following the grain of the fabric: 'finding the grain was tricky in this modern fabric, where the power of the loom has twisted the warp and weft'.[67] The maker's hands have power over the folds of silk, arbitrating between where the fabric is inclined to lie and the aesthetic preferences of the maker/client. Here, the maker's hands are mediators between textile and garment. Once satisfied that an accord has been reached, these pleats are basted (tacked) down using a long running stitch, which continues around the back to hold the rest of the lining piece to the outer textile. This is followed by a spaced backstitch, which is both decorative and holds the pleats in place. The rhythm of stitching again shifted: 'the stitch is swift, but there is a consciousness of the visibility of the tiny, raised blobs formed on the surface of the textile'.[68] As was observed in the brocade gown in the collection at Killerton, if this spaced backstitch is well executed, it can conceal myriad sins inside the gown.[69]

### 3.2.3 Constructing and Attaching the Fronts

The sewer then sets the backs aside, and turns attention to the fronts. In a busy mantuamaker's workshop with a myriad of making hands, these portions of the garment could be constructed simultaneously.[70] This is a key moment of divergence for bodice styles, dependent on the style of robings desired or, later in the century, whether it would be centre front closing. As the most common style examined, the recreation here will have single folded robings. Like the backs, this requires the lining piece to be placed on the fabric, several inches away from a selvedge edge (Video 4). The sewer then cuts the outer textile to mirror the lining, before extending the cut line in a rectangular shape over towards the selvedge edge. The selvedge can commonly be seen nestled within the robings on extant gowns. This cleverly makes use of a part of the textile that will not fray and therefore does not need additional hemming. This

---

[66] *Reflective Diary*, 30 January 2023.     [67] *Reflective Diary*, 31 January 2023.
[68] *Reflective Diary*, 31 January 2023.     [69] National Trust: NT 1360761.
[70] This is how the Isabella MacTavish Fraser Project gown was completed; see Rebecca Olds, "The Isabella Project," *Timesmith Dressmaking*. 2020, www.timesmith.co.uk/isabella-project. For a contemporary depiction of this kind of collaborative working, see Antoine Raspal, *A Sewing Workshop in Arles*, 1760, Musee Reattu.

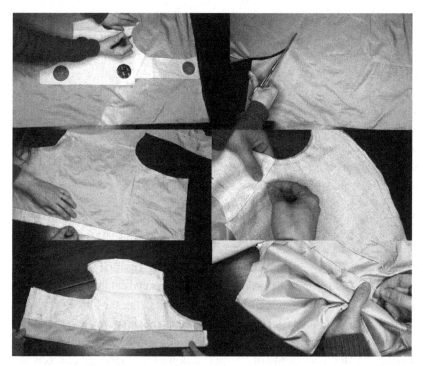

**Video 4** The process of cutting and stitching the front section of the gown, author's own footage. Video file available at www.cambridge.org/Dyer

selvedge edge is stitched down flat onto a strip of linen, which acts as a reinforcement to the robing, using a loose felling stitch. Hidden within the final gown, there is nothing to be gained from intricate stitching at this point: 'after the labour of the back pleats, the speed of this was very satisfying'.[71] Basted together into one piece, the sewer treats the lining and outer textile as one for the remainder of the construction process. Here, the sewer's fingers once again turn to pinching and pleating, as they manipulate first a small dart at the top of the bust, and then the robings into place:

> There are overlayed rhythms to this process. On the one hand, there is the rhythm of the stitch. Its tempo speeds up and slows, but it is a familiar procedure of piercing fabric and then pulling on the thread. But there is also a deeper beat which underlays the stitching, as hands move between sewing and manipulating the fabric. Those moments of directing and placing folds in the fabric are less structured, like bars of rest, allowing an interval in between the intensive moments of stitching.[72]

---

[71] *Reflective Diary*, 1 February 2023.    [72] *Reflective Diary*, 1 February 2023.

Once the fronts have been completed, the sewer must join the segments of the gown together. At the side seam, the sewer rolls back the seam allowance of the lining portion of the front, and layers it over the inside of the back piece, aligning the seamlines. All the layers are then stitched through with a felling stitch. The gown is then flipped over, and outer fabric stitched down by the sewer along the side seam with a spaced back stitch. Like the centre back, this is another pressure point, where the strain of wear could take its toll upon the gown. Instead of another intensely worked backstitch, the spaced backstitch and whipstitch work together to cooperatively reinforce each other, creating a strong and robust seam without unnecessarily piercing the silk.

### 3.2.4 Pleating and Attaching the Skirt

The skirts of the gown simultaneously present some of the simplest and some of the most critical hand labour within the gown. The first task is to stitch together the long seams of the skirt. Joined selvedge to selvedge, this seam is worked with a simple running stitch, and, despite being the longest seams in the gown, they are the fastest to sew: 'my hands move swiftly and rhythmically, and the gown suddenly feels large. The segments have abruptly all come together'.[73] But this rapidity of labour is followed by a moment of precision. An incision needs to be cut to divide the back of the bodice from the back of the skirts. Doing this incorrectly would be extremely costly, in terms of both the textile and the time spent on the labour. If the bodice lining shapes are cut accurately, however, then the cut simply needs to follow this line, curving down towards a point in the centre back. Here, the precise cutting knowledge of the sewer directly informs the success of the gown's construction later in the process.

Pleating the gown skirts up into the bodice is another area of ingenuity. The excess of the skirt fabric is folded right back under the back pleats, filling that voided space between the bottom of the bodice and the newly cut line at the top of the skirt (Video 5).[74] The pleats are approximated by eye, as was seen in the yellow gown at Leeds Museums and Galleries.[75] Frequently, extant gowns have an odd number of pleats on either side of the gown. The overall impression, rather than measured precision, was valued. This was also an area of trial and error: 'it took several attempts to get the pleats right, and it proved more

---

[73] *Reflective Diary*, 1 February 2023.

[74] Welborn provides a particularly effective explanation of this in *Introduction to Mantua-making: An 18th Century English Gown in Miniature* (online workshop, Burnley and Trowbridge, 2020).

[75] Leeds Museums and Galleries: LEEAG 2012.177.3.

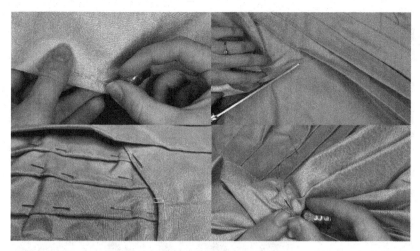

**Video 5** The process of pleating and attaching the skirt to the gown, author's own footage. Video file available at www.cambridge.org/Dyer

frustrating than any element so far'.[76] Once satisfied, the pleats were slotted between the lining and the outer textile and felled in place.

### 3.2.5 Making and Inserting the Sleeves

At this stage in the making, the gown appears to be near completion, but the sleeves present one of the lengthier components of the making process. In a collective mantuamakers' workspace, or even a familial collaboration within the home, the sleeves could be worked on by one maker in parallel with the labour outlined so far. Indeed, the process of making the sleeves and their cuffs takes a comparable amount of time to the main components of the gown already outlined. The core sleeve construction is creative and resourceful. Ingeniously, both the lining and outer textile are stitched together into a tube with a single row of stitching. The lining is rolled into a tube and placed on top of the outer textile, matching the back sleeve seam (Video 6). The sewer then temporarily tacks this tube in place with large, loose basting stitches, before laying the remaining outer textile over the top and, once again, using a spaced backstitch to hold everything in place. The tacking can then be removed. The sewer then turns in the raw edges at the cuff upon themselves, before finishing the edge with a running stitch, and overlaying the end of the sleeve with the cuff.

Cuff options are many on extant eighteenth-century gowns, and they were often a site of alteration, where changing fashions could be reflected with

---

[76] *Reflective Diary*, 1 February 2023.

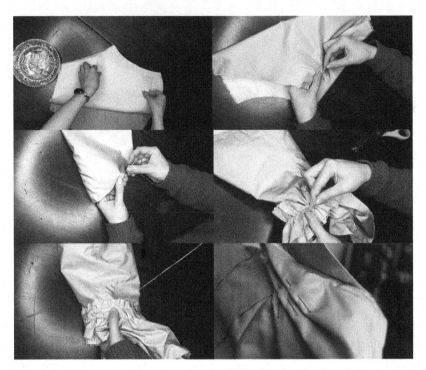

**Video 6** The process of constructing and inserting the sleeves, author's own footage. Video file available at www.cambridge.org/Dyer

minimal reworking of the gown itself.[77] The cuff constructed here echoed features of various cuffs, but predominantly mimicked the cuffs on the yellow gown at Leeds Museums and Galleries, which feature a double ruffle.[78] As with the extant example, the outer edges of each ruffle were finished with miniscule hems: 'keeping the hem even, especially as the fabric curved, required incredibly fine motor skills and haptic dexterity'.[79] The lower ruffle was, like the gown fronts, cut with the top edge on the selvedge to reduce the need for hemming, and this was then gathered up using a whip stitch, which is very similar to a felling stitch, but worked, in this case, over a single piece of fabric. The sewer then tacked this down to the bottom edge of the sleeve. The process was repeated with the upper cuff, which had its top edge pinked. Pinking is a process by which a metal stamp is used to cut a decorative edge into the fabric, preventing further fraying (Baumgarten, 1986, p. 25). The upper edge of

---

[77] For example, the pink and blue brocade gown described above displayed a later 1770s cuff on a 1760s-style gown. See Leeds Museums and Galleries: LEEAG 2012.177.1.

[78] Leeds Museums and Galleries: LEEAG 2012.177.3.    [79] *Reflective Diary*, 6 February 2023.

this outer layer was then box pleated (pleats alternated between facing left and right) in place and held in place with a running stitch.

The completed sleeves were then united with the rest of the gown. The lining of the shoulder strap was stitched to the back of the bodice, creating a circular opening for the arm. Under the arm, the curved portion of the sleeve was securely backstitched in place. The squared-off upper portion of the sleeve was then placed on top of the shoulder strap and pleated into place. This required some experimentation and, like the skirts, was done by eye. These pleats were tacked down and covered by the robings. Although this leaves an exposed raw edge, when worn, the tension of the body pulls the robings down on top of the sleeve head, concealing this unfinished textile. It is beneficial to conduct this on the body: 'without a body to work on, it is tricky to work out how much and where the fullness of the sleeve head needs to lie. There are so many considerations to keep in mind, from the range of movement of the wearer, to the need for a smooth, clean silhouette over the shoulder'.[80]

To complete the gown, the sewer turned up the hem and stitched it in place with a running stitch. Optional additions, such as a matching stomacher and petticoat, as well as further trim made from pinked strips of silk, were also stitched. These auxiliary elements were not filmed or recorded in the same way. They were not fundamental to gown construction, and, within an eighteenth-century context, may have been swapped in and out, altered, or replaced to update the effect of the gown itself. The gown was then complete.

### 3.2.6 Dressing the Body

The hand labour of eighteenth-century fashion cultures did not end when a gown was finished. Needles may be returned to their needle cases and spools of thread put away in workbags, but hands continued their sartorial work. The process of dressing extended many of the dexterous tasks and techniques of gown construction, and they were a core component of the diurnal rhythm of everyday life. Lacing, pinning, and tying, and, sometimes, even stitching continued to be enacted daily as part of the ritual of getting dressed.[81] Instead of distinct skills, there is a synchronous sartorial knowledge shared between the making and dressing hand.

On top of the linen shift, stays were laced closed over the body (Video 7). Eighteenth-century stay wearers did not aim to compress the waist, but instead to create a fashionable silhouette (Gernerd, 2023, pp. 151–187). The stays offered a firm canvas against which the rest of the gown could be pinned. Lacing them closed

---

[80] *Reflective Diary*, 6 February 2023.

[81] The engageantes (muslin sleeve ruffles) might be tacked onto a gown to allow both for easy laundering and so that a single set of embroidered ruffles might be worn with multiple gowns.

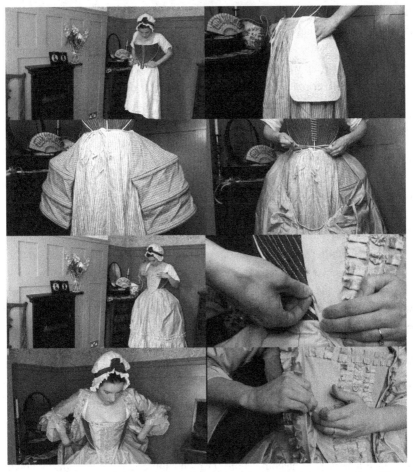

**Video 7** The process of getting dressed, author's own footage. Video file
available at www.cambridge.org/Dyer

brings to light another sartorial rhythm, as the hands move down the lacing cord,
encouraging it through each eyelet in succession. Next follows a succession of
tying, as the underpetticoat, pockets, panniers, and petticoat are layered up in
sequence. The wearer's hand then turns from tying to pinning. The stomacher is
pinned directly to the stays: 'there is no chance of reaching the skin beneath. The
baleen in the stays deflects each puncture like a sword blow glancing off armour.'[82]
Thrusting the pins downwards and embedding their tips within the fabric proved
remarkably sturdy. The gown was then donned like a coat and pinned to the
stomacher. Concealed under the robings, the angles of the pins did not need to be
uniform. The core principles of gown construction were extended here: that which

---

[82] *Reflective Diary*, 13 May 2023.

**Figure 22** The finished recreated gown, author's own image.

is concealed needs only be functional, that which is on show must appear precise and neat (Figure 22). Like the façade of an eighteenth-century building, the elegance of the exterior was a pretence which obscured the unsightly intricacies of construction.

## 3.3 Re-Embodying the Maker: Temporality, Gesture, and Bodies

As Amanda Card has argued, 'bodies are research tools', but care is required (Card, 2019). The normative practices of the body are particular to the time, place, and social and cultural structures it inhabits. Experimental attempts to embody past practices can only ever be partial. Yet mobilising the body as a research tool and attempting to capture some sense of gesture, movement, and practice reveals slivers of information about the past which are absent from other modes of historical enquiry (Johnson, 2015; Davidson, 2019). Conclusions must be couched against these limitations, but they can be rich and transformative in shaping how the past is interpreted. In another experiment, for example, I have worn stays while stitching a gown, and found that the supportive nature of the stays eliminated the back pain felt when the same tasks were carried out in modern clothing.[83] These shards of recaptured, experiential knowledge do not pretend to allow a full re-inhabitation of the past (Dupré et al., 2020). Instead, they illuminate those tacit aspects of practice which are lost in text and ignite sparks of possibility and insight.

The temporalities of making and remaking which are revealed via this re-embodiment process are complex. A practiced and seasoned mantuamaker would have likely been able to produce a gown at a greater speed than any modern maker, so attempts to uncover how long it might have taken to make a gown through recreation will prove loose at best. Perhaps more fruitful is an appreciation of the rhythms of making, whatever their relative tempo. As Nithikul Nimkilrat has stated, there is 'a rhythmic interplay between bodily and thinking practices' when the researcher engages in recreative practices (2010, p. 77). One of the terms frequently repeated throughout my reflective diary was 'rhythm'. The pace and beats of that rhythm were fluid, but there was a pattern, and an ebb and flow, between different stages of making. This rhythm was articulated through gesture: piercing the fabric with the needle, followed by the stretching of the arm as it draws the thread through the textile, or the gentle easing and smoothing of pleats with the twist of the wrist. Attached to this rhythm was a dominant emphasis on efficiency. Time was fundamental to the value of commodified labour, and there is an omnipresent interplay between the efficacy of the stitching in terms of the relative robustness of the sewing, and the time it would take to complete (Thompson, 1967; Voth, 2000; Dyer, 2021). There is an intentionality and economy behind that ingenious balance between speed and quality.

The sense of synergy extends to the relationship between the body, its gestures, and the tools used in the sewing process. At points, the body itself felt as if it had transmogrified into a sewing tool: 'my fingers feel like a multi-tool, transforming from implements of stitching into an iron and back again'.[84] This fluidity and flexibility of utility was powerfully self-reliant. Somatic memory was also generated through these repeated manual tasks, in terms of both producing an automated regularity within the stitching, and an intuitive knowledge when feeling how and where pleats should be placed and fall (Smith, 2012). The only way to know was to do, and the hand learnt without the direction of my conscious mind. Yet, conversely, the mind was also constantly aware of and observant of how different stages in the construction process

---

[83] Experiment carried out at Jane Austen's House, Chawton, 21 June 2023.
[84] *Reflective Diary*, 2 February 2023.

would interweave. The positioning of the centre back seam, for example, was crucial to how the finished gown would look, as was the placement of the back pleats so that they lined up with the robings where they met at the shoulder. While the hands themselves were dexterous tools, their relationship with the practical non-bodily tools of sewing completed this cooperative interaction between the sewing mind and body. The thimble, which is worn on the middle finger of the dominant sewing hand, offers vital armour to the hands as it propels the needle through the textile. It protects the hand and speeds up the process.

Hands, tools, and gesture worked together in eighteenth-century gown construction, keeping time with familiar rhythms of manual labour. Ingenuity and efficiency dominated mantuamaking practice, as methods prioritised speed and demonstrated intimate and anatomical awareness of the needs of the clothed body. The commercial nature of eighteenth-century consumer cultures also tightened its grasp around the methods of mantuamaking, as the economic value of labour drove decisions around the efficacy and productivity of the sewing hand (McKendrick, 1982). Mantuamaking acts as a microcosm of eighteenth-century fashionable and commercial life, wedding the importance of external appearances with the financial pressures of a consumer society. Stitching wrought more than gowns, it fashioned in textiles the cultural and operational structures of sartorial cultures.

## 4 The Manual Labour of Style

The completion of a garment – stitched, pinned, and worn on the body – did not mark the end of its life. Hand labour extended beyond these moments of garment making and dressing to create and maintain broader cultures of sartorial style. Fashion cultures were created by garments worn on the body, the hands of their makers, and other diverse (often paper-based) fashionable practices. The stitching hand was accompanied by hands which painted, engraved, wrote about, and otherwise wrought sartorial style in Georgian England. These additional hand skills, while not integral to the making of fashionable garments themselves, played vital roles in the generation and development of fashion as a cultural phenomenon. Hand labours contextualised garments, imbuing them with power, significance, and influence. It was via these fashionably attentive hands that styles were disseminated, sartorial literacy expressed, and fashionability performed.

These various sartorial hands which shaped women's fashion cultures did not all belong to women. Apart from the tailors who made riding habits and staymakers, women's fashionable dress was predominantly stitched by women. However, the hands which drew, engraved, and wrote about women's fashions were mobilised by both men and women of various sartorial experiences and backgrounds. Here, intriguing dynamics between varieties of creative labour emerge. The roles of designer and fabricator, so often more clearly delineated in contemporary fashion cultures, were more fluid. It is unclear from where creative genius sprang: the hands which stitched or those that drew. Collaborative endeavour, entrepreneurial experiment, and mutability of approach appear to dominate the broader cultures of hand labour in fashion.

## 4.1 Fashion Engraved

The dissemination of fashion radically transformed in the eighteenth century, in both text and image. Prior to the eighteenth century, fashion travelled via sight, sporadic reports, and devices such as the fashion doll (Peers, 2004; Nachman, 2014; Pitman, 2022). Seventeenth-century engraved images, known as 'costume prints', had anticipated the use of print to circulated fashion (Wilson, 2005; Rublack, 2015). These retrospective images presented recent fashions, with distinctions drawn along national and cultural lines. Their purpose was ethnographical and centred on the development of sartorial literacy and social distinction, rather than expressly to disseminate new styles which might be copied and worn. Many of the functions and limitations of the seventeenth-century 'costume print' carried over into the earliest forms of fashion plate which circulated in the eighteenth century. These early fashion plates were compressed into a tiny, pocket-sized format, they were monochrome, and they lacked any detail or explanation. They appeared in pocket books, which were a 'hybrid genre' included a consistent set of basic elements: diary pages, an accounting section, and an array of tables containing valuable information (Colclough, 2015). As Jennie Batchelor states, pocket books were published under a proliferation of 'bewilderingly similar titles', and they enjoyed a diverse readership (2003, p. 4; Leis, 2013). The fashion plate was a feminising addition to these small portable diaries, which were used to distinguish the ladies' pocket book from those for children or men (Dyer, 2022). They usually appeared next to other, larger engravings, which might illustrate some other element of the publication, positioning fashion as part of a broader cultural literacy (Figure 23).

These images, however, were stymied in their utility as fashion disseminators, due to a major temporal shortcoming, as *The Magazine á la Mode* explained in 1777:

**Figure 23** A lady in the newest full dress and another in the most fashionable undress, *The Ladies New and Polite Pocket Memorandum-book*, 1777. Courtesy of the Folger Shakespeare Library.

> For some years past, annual Pocket-Books have [pretended] to convey an idea of the reigning mode of dress . . . of the current year. The futility of such pretensions must be obvious to every one who gives himself time to reflect, that nothing is more variable than fashions in dress, and that any one mode of dress is so far from being likely to continue a whole year, that very probably, it may not last a month.[85]

Fashion plates within pocket books appeared only once each year, and depicted the fashions of the previous year. This retrospective delay or, as Batchelor as term it, 'sartorial insufficiency', was satirised by Oliver Goldsmith in his 1773 play: *She Stoops to Conquer* (Batchelor, 2003, p. 12). When Hastings questions the fashionability of Mrs Hardcastle's hair, she protests: 'I dressed it myself from a print in the Ladies Memorandum Book for the last year' (Goldsmith, 1773, II, i, p. 39. The sartorial languor within the publishing profession was gradually corrected, as women's monthly periodicals increasingly picked up pace in the latter decades of the century. Following an abortive attempt from its namesake in the 1750s, the *Lady's Magazine* (1770–1847) began sporadically including fashion plates from the 1770s (Batchelor, 2022; Smith, 2013; Smith, 2018). It is no coincidence that this was the same decade that newspapers also began to regularly and rapaciously spread news of the latest fashions worn by the London elite (Greig, 2015; Gernerd, 2023, pp. 24, 31). From the 1770s onwards, comparable prints appeared across Europe in Jacque Esnaut and

---

[85] *The Magazine a la Mode*, I, 3 January 1777.

Michel Rapilly's *Galerie des Modes* (1778–1787), *Journal der Luxus und der Moden* (1786–1826), *Journal für Fabrik, Manufaktur und Handlung und Mode* (1791–1808), and Nicolaus Heideloff's *Gallery of Fashion* (1794–1802) (Langley Moore, 1971; McNeil and Steorn, 2013; Calahan, 2015). By the turn of the nineteenth century, the fashion plate was a ubiquitous and crucial feature of fashion cultures.

While historians have considered the function of these images once they were completed and placed within the pages of pocket books and periodicals, the authorship of the fashion plate has remained relatively obscure. Peter McNeil and Patrik Steorn have highlighted Polish-German artist Daniel Nikolaus Chodowiecki as being an influential hand in shaping the fashion plate across Europe (McNeil and Steorn, 2013). While artists like Chodowiecki reiterated fashions that they observed, *Gallery of Fashion* explicitly credited the garments depicted to ladies of the British elite, although the identity of the artist and engraver is less explicit:

> Several Ladies of rank and fashion have not only approved of this plan, but they have at the same time granted permission to the Publisher to make drawings of their new dresses, and to insert them in this GALLERY; thus the credit of the invention of the different dresses, will be secured to those Fair Subscribers who contribute to the embellishment of this work … And they will find the Publisher always ready to represent their dresses in that style of elegance, and that original taste, which is so peculiar to the British Ladies.[86]

By the early decades of the nineteenth century *La Belle Assemblée* (1805–1832) routinely credited its fashion plates to Margaret Lanchester, who had previously overseen *Le Miroir de la Mode* (1803–1804), and later Mary Anne Bell (*née* Millard), while the *Lady's Magazine* followed suit in 1818, attributing their fashion plate designs to Miss Macdonald of 50 South Moulton Street, Bond Street (Batchelor, 2022, p. 190; Phillips, 2006, pp. 175–179). Macdonald was later replaced by Mrs W Smith of 15 Old Burlington Street, before eventually the magazine eventually committed to relying on the designs of Miss Pierpoint, of 12 Edward Street, Portman Square, after 1823. These women were almost exclusively mantuamakers (more commonly known as dressmakers by the early decades of the nineteenth century), and their designs were likely wrought with needles rather than pencils and paints. Their acknowledgement explicitly linked print cultures with the commercial cultures of fashion, encouraging periodical consumers to become garment consumers.

The collaborative nature of the transition from garment to print is illuminated through the example of Lanchester's work with *La Belle Assemblée*. Here,

---

[86] *Gallery of Fashion* (London, 1794–1802), I, 1.

varieties of manual labour come together to see the fashion plate imagined, drawn, engraved, and published. An 1806 plate in *La Belle Assemblée* depicting fashionable dress for spring was 'drawn by Mr. Devis, from the elegant Designs of Madame Lanchester'.[87] Arthur William Devis (1762–1822) was an artist and engraver, who was responsible for drawing numerous illustrations for periodicals in this period and enjoyed success as a society portrait painter.[88] In 1806, Devis married Lanchester, and the newlyweds combined both their households and their professional skillsets, echoing the collaborative marriage of printmaker couple the Darlys in the 1770s (Paviere, 1937; Gernerd, 2020). This collaboration enacted an alliance between the sartorial and artistic worlds. Lanchester plied her scissors and needle, and her husband applied his pencil and paints, and together the two varieties of hand skill combined to generate a vehicle for the promotion of both forms of manual labour. A sketch by Devis from 1814 (Figure 24) displays several of the compositional and structural features of the fashion plate, from the figure's classicised facial features and scattering of contextual interior elements to the placement of the mirror, which allowed both the front and back of the garment to be displayed. The mirror was a regular conceit in fashion plates, which circumvented many of the restrictions incumbent on transforming three-dimensional dress into a two-dimensional image (Figure 25). This sartorial consciousness echoes the symbiosis between hand and mind observed in sewing practices and speaks to the synergy between sartorial and broader artistic practice in the period.

Acknowledgement of the design and drawing of these images of fashion only traces the journey from garment to printed page part way. Once drawn, that image was then passed to an engraver, such as James Heath (1757–1834), who translated the pencil lines into etched imprints on the copper plates which give the fashion plate its name (Fordham and Albright, 2012). Heath conducted much of the engraving for *Lady's Magazine* and, like Devis and Lanchester, consolidated this professional relationship through his daughter Charlotte's marriage to the magazine's editor, Samuel Hamilton (Batchelor, 2022, p. 175). This familial and close-knit community brought together the interconnected threads of sartorial manual labour, and this was reflected in the familial

---

[87] *La Belle Assemblée* (London, May 1806). Other artists, like Thomas Uwins, designed the fashion plates for Rudolph Ackermann's *Repository of Arts*. The complete set of original drawings by Thomas Uwins of fashion plates for the *Repository* was sold by Kerry Taylor Auctions on 17 June 2019, lot 36.

[88] For his prints, see for example, Victoria and Albert Museum: S.530-2011; S.3171-2013. Devis also painted *Death of Nelson* (1805); see Royal Maritime Museum, Greenwich: BHC2894. Through the 1780s he was a portrait artist in India, where he painted East India Company officials, such as William Monson and His Wife, Ann Debonnaire (c. 1786), see Los Angeles County Museum of Art: 47.29.16.

**Figure 24** Arthur William Devis, *A Sketch After Nature*, 1814. Victoria and
Albert Museum, E.862-1939.

networks via which such skills were routinely learnt and spread (Lyons, 2024).
This array of interconnected hands worked in alliance across an array of
mediums to translate, transform, and transfer knowledge of fashionable dress.
This process of translation from garment to drawing to engraving to print can
also be viewed through the lens of remaking. While remaking garments was
centred on keeping in step with the changing styles of fashion, that temporal

**Figure 25** Evening full dress in April 1809, *La Belle Assemblée*, 1809. University of Otago, New Zealand.

rhythm was set by these printed images, which were themselves sequential remakings across their respective mediums. Garments passed through many hands and many formats as their fashionability was established.

The fashion plate has been elevated as an arbiter of fashion, but the authorship of those images often remains obscure. While it is occasionally possible to trace the connections between the various makers' hands which contributed to an image, especially in the early decades of the nineteenth century, this is still relatively rare amongst the hundreds of such images that exist from the eighteenth century. The authorship of most fashion plates went uncredited, especially prior to the rise of the periodical fashion plate from the 1770s. Where provenance can be identified, it is collaborative and composite, drawing together the hand skills of mantuamakers, artists, engravers, and printers. These hands have been routinely credited with immense power over fashion change. Doris Langley Moore stated that the fashion plate's only purpose was to 'create a favourable climate of opinion' for the latest styles (1971, p. 10). While the fashion plate is certainly more than a sartorial ambassador, the commercial dimension of the later prints frames the fashion plate as a marketing device devised to promote both mantuamaker and publisher. More broadly, such images set the temporal rhythms of the fashion, from the annual progress of the pocket book to the monthly periodicals of the nineteenth century. As intersecting modes of manual labour, sewing, drawing, and printmaking worked in uneasy unison to generate the temporal notions of fashion change which drove sartorial cultures.

## 4.2 Fashion, Creativity, and Craft

The reception of the fashion plate, and indeed fashion more broadly, was not passive. The fashion consumer presents a further agent for manual creativity, further breaking down binary distinctions between makers and consumers (Dyer, 2020). Hand work not only crafted dress, but it also acted as an indicator of fashionable membership, knowledge, and ability. Genteel women performed their fashionability through the work of their hands, both through Smith's articulation of the hand as a site of social performance, and through the works created by those hands, whether via watercolours, their own textile crafts, or the accumulation and presentation of albums (Smith, 2014; Dyer, 2021). As a penultimate reflection within this Element, consideration will turn to how these creative modes of fashionable craft extended the role of hands and hand making within eighteenth-century cultures of fashion production beyond the production and acquisition of garments.

Fashion plates often provided the vehicle for creative and artistic responses to fashion cultures. Bluestocking Mary Berry (1763–1852) and her sister, Agnes (1764–1852) were the agents behind one of the more unusual uses of fashion plate images. In 1801, Berry staged a production of her play, *Fashionable Friends*, at Horace Walpole's Strawberry Hill in 1801 (Schmid, 2012). To plan out the staging, Berry prepared an album of watercolour sets in miniature. These stage sets were populated by twenty-nine figures cut from the fashion plates of *Gallery of Fashion*, who stood in for the play's characters.[89] Careful and dexterous cutting was required to free these figures from the page, as the scissors deftly navigated the curling corners of ostrich feathers and the delicate lines of diaphanous 1790s gowns. This application of the images also speaks to the relative value placed upon them. While the publication was expensive, the Berry sisters seem to have been unreserved in their willingness to obliterate the pages of this pricey publication, and perceived the value of the figures to be in their resemblance to the elite women who would perform the play (Engel, 2011). Here, creativity with the materials of fashionable dissemination also connected to broader creative forms of literature and performance.

Fashion plates also offered an opportunity for creative manual interactions with fashion via the work of copying. Some of these copies were precise replicas, while others were creative reinterpretations. The fashion plate could

---

[89] The album is now in a private collection, but one scene has been reproduced (Elliot, 2019, p. 59).

**Figure 26** January 1814 Promenade Dress, watercolour. Private collection.

offer a model for watercolour practice, positioning fashion within the skills of accomplishment beyond needlework. For example, a copy of the 'promenade dress' from the January 1814 issue of the *Repository of Arts* (Figures 26 and 27) demonstrates how the fashion plate can act as an artistic model. This image was a retrospective copy, rather than part of the creative process undertaken by the *Repository*'s fashion plate artist, Thomas Uwins.[90] In this copy, the hand of the watercolourist is naïve and unpractised. Yet the sartorial details are carefully and faithfully mimicked. Perhaps most impressive was the artist's exact replication of the pelisse coat's warm golden yellow colour. This process of copying was fundamental to genteel girls' education as they developed the accomplishment of drawing. Engravings were regularly used as the models for these

---

[90] The original design for this plate by Thomas Uwins was sold by Kerry Taylor Auctions on 17 June 2019, lot 36.

**Figure 27** Promenade Dress, January 1814, from the *Repository of Arts*. Los Angeles County Museum of Art.

educational practices (Bermingham, 2000, pp. 149–155). Other genteel water-colourists used fashion plates as a compositional and stylistic model in their own artistic endeavours. Ann Frankland Lewis (1757–1842) created 'dress of the year' watercolours from her teens through to her fifties, echoing the temporal and historicising power of the fashion plate generated in the annual pocket book prints to mark the passing of time (Dyer, 2021, pp. 49–122).[91]

Other genteel and fashionably engaged women grasped not their pens and paintbrushes, but their scissors and needles. Fanny Austen Knight (1793–1882), the niece of the famed novelist Jane Austen, was gifted a copy of the *Ladies Complete Pocket Book* in 1804.[92] Knight used the pocket book avidly, following

[91] For the original paintings, see Los Angeles County Museum of Art: AC1999.154.1-.32.
[92] Kent Archives: U951/F24/1-69.

its conventions by entering purchases of sweets and ribbons in the little volume's accounting pages. However, she also took a more creative approach. The fashion plates in Knight's 1804 and 1805 editions of the pocket book were 'dressed'. Dressed prints were engravings where portions of the figures' clothing (and occasionally upholstery) were carefully cut away and replaced with a textile (Dyer, 2021, pp. 131–39). The process was intricate, and highly skilled examples retain minuscule slivers of the print to act as outlines and details.[93] Knight's attempts were naïve, but lack of skill does not equate to a less valuable articulation of intent. Eleven-year-old Knight strove to engage with the fashionable world she was on the cusp of entering, expressing her material literacy through her matching of garments with appropriate textiles, even if her precision with the scissors was lacking.

Creative engagement with the cultures of fashion is also evident in album culture. Barbara Johnson's well-known album aligned fashion plates with fabric samples from her own gowns, while the nineteenth century saw the practice of collecting scraps of textile evolve as a form of personal and group biography (Rothstein, 1987; Dyer, 2019a, 2021; Strasdin, 2023). Catherine Hutton (1756–1846) approached the collation of fashion plates as a historical endeavour (Dyer, 2021). Although the album is now lost, Hutton wrote about her practice in her memoirs, where she stated that her collection of '650 English figures and 782 foreign' would 'constitute a history of the habits of this country' (1891, pp. 214–16). Interspersed with some ethnographic costume prints and drawings taken from other sources, fashion plates were here mobilised as historical record, generating an archive of fashion cultures and presented as capsules of sartorial style. Akin to dressed prints, Hutton describes how she carefully cut out each print in a uniform fashion, before pasting them inside the album alongside her written narrative of sartorial history. Fashion – whether in paper or textile form – was central to creative manual production beyond the walls of the mantuamaker's shop.

## 4.3 The Maker's Hand

Hands made clothes in the eighteenth century, but they also acted as a point of connection and assemblage between the diverse manual activities which fabricated the broader cultures of fashion. Fashion news was fundamental to the developing sartorial cultures of the latter half of the century: it was pivotal in speeding up fashion's rhythms, driving consumer demand, and providing a forum for new inventions and innovations in style. Similarly, the creative accomplishments of genteel women and girls extended those tactile practices within domestic spaces. Whether professional or amateur, wielding needle or

---

[93] See, for example, Sabine Winn's dressed prints, National Trust: NT960084.

paint brush, it was hands which drove the powerful commercial and cultural force of fashion.

This Element has focused on women's fashionable dress in eighteenth-century England, but its arguments extend beyond those categories. A web of handmaking connects genders, crafts, and nations. Men, as well as women and girls, enjoyed a material literacy around their clothes and, while not as closely involved in its construction, some turned their own hands to making and mending (Styles, 2007, p. 156). Other making activities, like concocting pomades, powders, and cosmetics, might also take place within the home and have occupied many busy hands (Burke, 2023). Neither were the tensions between industry and craft confined to England, nor Britain. Proponents of industrialisation and mechanisation also remained aware of the importance of hands to crank winches, operate looms, and work mines. 'The devil makes work for idle hands' was first set down in that recognisable form in the eighteenth century (Coster, 2016, p. 94). Productivity and personal value rested upon the hand, at whatever task it laboured.

Whether working in a factory or stitching a gown in a genteel parlour, hands were a fundamental mediator between the human body and the material and natural world. As Pamela Smith has argued, 'the work of the human hand' allowed natural philosophers to succeed in 'harnessing nature' (2006, p. 91). This extended beyond the scientific realms of philosophy and into the material and commercial world of fashion. To modern-day consumers, garments often feel far removed from the natural world, yet each fibre, every atom of a gown in the eighteenth century was grown and harvested, whether from silkworms, cotton, or flax plants (Fennetaux and Mentges, 2022). Hands were the intermediaries, which processed and manipulated the products of the natural world to suit the needs of human bodies.

The labour behind processes of making was sensorily rich and culturally framed. Recreative approaches to history, as this Element has demonstrated, offer an opportunity to graze against the ghostly hands of the past. The researcher's hands cannot fully inhabit those of the eighteenth-century maker, but they can trace their movements, track their activities, and edge closer to an understanding of the embodied experiences and processes of labour. Manual labour was inherently physical. It relied on haptic experience to carry out, replicate, and improve upon its practices. It may only be possible to grasp at phantoms of past bodily practise, but there is potential to get closer via recreation than by means of texts, objects, and images alone. Cultures of sartorial handiwork were nuanced, but they were primarily experienced and understood through the hands. Sewing was sensory, bodily, and manual. As eighteenth-century fashion cultures were connected and allied through the movements and practices of the skilled hand, so too can researchers access the making skill of the past through the labour of their own hands.

# References

## Primary Printed Sources

Campbell, R. (1747) *The London Tradesman*. London: T. Gardener.

Diderot, D. (1763) *Encyclopédie, ou dictionnaire raisonné des sciences, des arts et des métiers*. Paris.

Garsault, F. (1769) *L'Art du Tailleur*. Paris.

Goldsmith, O. (1773) *She Stoops to Conquer; or, the Mistakes of a Night*. London: E. Newbery.

Gurney, J. (1768) *The Trial of Frederick Calvert*. Dublin: Mein & Fleeming.

Holme, R. (1688) *The Academy of Armoury*. Chester.

Hutton, C. (1891) *Reminiscences of a Gentlewoman of the Last Century*, ed. Catherine Beale. Birmingham: Cornish Brothers.

Stuart, L. (1895) *Gleanings from an Old Portfolio, 1785–1799*, ed. Godfrey Clark. Edinburgh: D. Douglas.

Trench, M. (1862) *The Remains of the Late Mrs Richard Trench: Being Selections from Her Journals, Letters, & Other Papers*. London: Parker, Son, and Bourn.

## Secondary Sources

Abrams, L. and Gardner, L. (2021) 'Recognising the Co-dependence of Machine and Hand in the Scottish Knitwear Industry', *Textile History*, 52 (1–2), pp. 165–189.

Adamson, G. (2013) *The Invention of Craft*. London: Bloomsbury.

Allen, R. C. (2009) *The British Industrial Revolution in Global Perspective*. Cambridge: Cambridge University Press.

Anishanslin, Z. (2016) *Portrait of a Woman in Silk: Hidden Histories of the British Atlantic World*. London: Yale University Press.

Arnold, J. (1989) *Patterns of Fashion 1: The Cut and Construction of Women's Dress, 1660–1860*. London: Macmillan.

Arnold, J. et al. (2021) *Patterns of Fashion 1: The Cut and Construction of Women's Dress, 1660–1860*. London: School of Historical Dress.

Barker, M. (2021) *c.1760s Yellow Night-Gown Handbook*. Surbiton: Grosvenor House Publishing.

Batchelor, J. (2003) 'Fashion and Frugality: Eighteenth-Century Pocket Books for Women', *Studies in Eighteenth Century Culture*, 32, pp. 1–18.

Batchelor, J. (2005) *Dress, Distress and Desire: Clothing and the Female Body in Eighteenth-Century Literature*. London: Palgrave.

Batchelor, J. (2022) *The Lady's Magazine (1770–1832) and the Making of Literary History*. Edinburgh: Edinburgh University Press. https://doi.org/10.1515/9781474487665.

Baudino, I. and Carré, J. (eds.) (2005) *The Invisible Woman: Aspects of Women's Work in Eighteenth-Century Britain*. Abingdon: Routledge.

Baumgarten, L. (1986) *Eighteenth-Century Clothing at Williamsburg*. Williamsburg: Colonial Williamsburg Foundation.

Baumgarten, L. (2002) *What Clothes Reveal: The Language of Clothing in Colonial and Federal America*. New York: Yale University Press.

Beaudry, M. C. (2006) *Findings: The Material Culture of Needlework and Sewing*. London: Yale University Press.

Bendall, S. A. (2019) 'The Case of the "French Vardinggale": A Methodological Approach to Reconstructing and Understanding Ephemeral Garments', *Fashion Theory*, 23(3), pp. 363–399.

Bendall, S. A. (2021a) *Shaping Femininity: Foundation Garments, the Body and Women in Early Modern England*. London: Bloomsbury.

Bendall, S. A. (2021b) 'Women's Dress and the Demise of the Tailoring Monopoly: Farthingale-Makers, Body-Makers and the Changing Textile Marketplace of Seventeenth-Century London', *Textile History*, 52(1–2), pp. 23–55.

Bendall, S. A. (2022) 'The Queens' Dressmakers: Women's Work and the Clothing Trades in Late Seventeenth-Century London', *Women's History Review*, 32(3), pp. 389–414.

Bermingham, A. (2000) *Learning to Draw: Studies in the Cultural History of a Polite and Useful Art*. London: Yale University Press.

Birt, S. (2021) 'Women, Guilds and the Tailoring Trades: The Occupational Training of Merchant Taylors' Company Apprentices in Early Modern London', *London Journal*, 46(2), pp. 146–164.

Bradfield, N. (1968) *Costume in Detail, 1730–1930*. Barming: Eric Dobby.

Buck, A. (1979) *Dress in Eighteenth Century England*. London: Batsford.

Burgio, L., Domoney K., Haseldine, G., and McCaffrey-Howarth C. (2023) 'Making London Porcelain – A Multidisciplinary Project Connecting Local Communities with the Technological and Innovation Histories of London's Early Porcelain Manufacturers', *Heritage* 6(2), pp. 1958–1976.

Burke, J. (2023) *How to Be a Renaissance Woman: An Untold History of Beauty and Female Creativity*. London: Profile.

Burman, B. and Fennetaux, A. (2019) *The Pocket: A Hidden History of Women's Lives, 1660–1900*. London: Yale University Press.

Cabell, E. K. (1988) *Women Merchants and Milliners in Eighteenth Century Williamsburg*. Williamsburg, VA: Colonial Williamsburg Foundation.

Calahan, A. (2015). Fashion Plates: 150 Years of Style. New Haven: Yale University Press.

Callaghan, E. (1999) 'What is Experimental Archaeology?', in Westcott, D. (ed.) *Primitive Technology: A Book of Earth Skills*. Layton: Gibbs Smith, pp. 4–6.

Card, A. (2019) 'Body and Embodiment', in Agnew, V., Lamb, J., and Tomann, J. (eds.) *The Routledge Handbook of Reenactment Studies: Key Terms in the Field*. London: Routledge, pp. 30–33.

Chang, H. (2016) *Autoethnography as Method*. London: Routledge.

Chrisman-Campbell, K. (2015) *Fashion Victims: Dress at the Court of Louis XVI and Marie-Antoinette*. London: Yale University Press.

Colclough, S. (2015) 'Pocket Books and Portable Writing: The Pocket Memorandum Book in Eighteenth-Century England and Wales', *The Yearbook of English Studies*, 45, pp. 159–177.

Coster, W. (2016) *Family and Kinship in England 1450-1800*. London: Taylor and Francis.

Cox, A. and Stowell L. (2017) *The American Duchess Guide to Eighteenth-Century Dressmaking*. Salem: Page Street Press.

Davidson, H. (2015) 'Reconstructing Jane Austen's Silk Pelisse, 1812-1814', *Costume*, 49(2), pp. 198–223.

Davidson, H. (2019) 'The Embodied Turn: Making and Remaking Dress as an Academic Practice', *Fashion Theory*, 23(3), pp. 329–362.

De Vries, J. (2008) *The Industrious Revolution: Consumer Behaviour and the Household Economy, 1650 – Present*. Cambridge: Cambridge University Press.

Dormer, P. (ed.) (1997) *The Culture of Craft*. Manchester: Manchester University Press.

Dowdell, C. (2010) *The Fruits of Nimble Fingers: Garment Construction and the Working Lives of Eighteenth-Century English Needlewomen*. MA thesis, University of Alberta.

Dowdell, C. (2017) 'Gertrude Savile's Green Damask: A Case Study of Clothing Reuse and Alteration in Eighteenth-Century England', *Clothing Cultures*, 4(1), pp. 29–44.

Dowdell, C. (2021) 'No Small Share of Ingenuity': An Object-Oriented Analysis of Eighteenth-Century English Dressmaking, *Costume*, 55(2), pp. 186–211.

Dupré, S. Harris, A. Kursell, J. Lulof, P. and M. Stols-Witlox (eds.) (2020) *Reconstruction, Replication and Re-enactment in the Humanities and Social Sciences*. Amsterdam: Amsterdam University Press.

Dyer, S. (2019a) 'Barbara Johnson's Album: Material Literacy and Consumer Practice, 1746–1823', *Journal for Eighteenth-Century Studies*, 42(3), pp. 263–282.

Dyer, S. (2020) '"Magnificent as well as Singular": Hester Thrale's Polynesian Court Dress of 1781', in *Fashion and Authorship: Literary Production and Cultural Style from the Eighteenth to the Twenty-First Century*. London: Palgrave Macmillan, pp. 43–62.

Dyer, S. (2020) 'Stitching and Shopping: The Material Literacy of the Consumer', in Dyer, S. and Smith, C. W. (eds.) *Material Literacy in Eighteenth-Century Britain*. London: Bloomsbury, pp. 99–116.

Dyer, S. (2021) *Material Lives: Women Makers and Consumer Culture in the 18th Century*. London: Bloomsbury.

Dyer, S. (2022) 'Fashions of the Day: Materiality, Temporality and the Fashion Plate, 1750–1879', in Dyer, S., Halbert, J., and Littlewood, S. (eds.) *Disseminating Dress: Britain's Fashion Networks, 1600–1970*. London: Bloomsbury, pp. 73–94.

Dyer, S. and Smith, C. W. (eds.) (2020) *Material Literacy in Eighteenth-Century Britain: A Nation of Makers*. London: Bloomsbury.

Earle, P. (1989) 'The Female Labour Market in London in the Late Seventeenth and Early Eighteenth Centuries', *The Economic History Review*, 42(3), pp. 328–353.

Elliot, P. (2019) *Cut and Paste: 400 Years of Collage*. Edinburgh: National Galleries Scotland.

Engel, L. (2011) *Fashioning Celebrity: Eighteenth-Century British Actresses and Strategies for Image Making*. Columbus: Ohio State University Press.

Fennetaux, A., Junqua, A., and Vasset, S. (eds.) (2014) *The Afterlife of Used Things: Recycling in the Long Eighteenth Century*. London: Routledge.

Fennetaux, A. and Mentges, G., (2022) 'Introduction: parure, culture et nature — vers une écologie matérielle du vêtement', *Apparence(s)*, 11, online only.

Fordham, D., & Albright, A. (2012). The Eighteenth-Century Print: Tracing the Contours of a Field. Literature Compass, 9(8), 509–520.

Frye, S. (2011) *Pens and Needles: Women's Textualities in Early Modern England*. Philadelphia: University of Pennsylvania Press.

Gardner, L. (2019) *Mechanising the Needle: The Development of the Sewing Machine as a Manufacturing Tool, 1851-1980*. PhD thesis, University of Glasgow.

Gernerd, E. (2020). Fancy Feathers: The feather trade in Britain and the Atlantic World. In S. Dyer & C. W. Smith (Eds.), Material Literacy in Eighteenth-Century Britain (pp. 195–217). London: Bloomsbury.

Gernerd, E. (2023) *The Modern Venus: Dress, Underwear and Accessories in the Late 18th-Century Atlantic World*. London: Bloomsbury.

Gerritsen, A. and Riello, G. (eds.) (2015) *Writing Material Culture History*. London: Bloomsbury.

Ginsburg, M. (1972) 'The Tailoring and Dressmaking Trades, 1700–1850', *Costume*, 6(1), pp. 64–71. https://doi.org/10.1179/cos.1972.6.1.64.

Gowing, L. (2021) *Ingenious Trade: Women and Work in Seventeenth-Century London*. Cambridge: Cambridge University Press.

Greig, H. (2015) 'Faction and Fashion: The Politics of Court Dress in Eighteenth-Century England', *Apparences*, 6.

Haru Crowston, C. (2001) *Fabricating Women: The Seamstresses of Old Regime France, 1675–1791*. London: Duke University Press.

Harvey, K. (ed.) (2009) *History and Material Culture*. London: Routledge.

Harvey, K. (2016) 'Craftsmen in Common: Objects, Skills and Masculinity in the Eighteenth and Nineteenth Centuries', in Greig, H., Hamlett, J., and Hannan, L. (eds.) *Gender and Material Culture in Britain since 1600*. London: Palgrave, pp. 68–89.

Heath, C., Hindmarsh, J., and Luff, P. (2010) *Video in Qualitative Research*. New York: Sage.

Hill, B. (2005) *Women, Work and Sexual Politics in Eighteenth-Century England*. London: Routledge.

Hodge, S. (2012) *Why Your Five-Year-Old Could Not Have Done That: Modern Art Explained*. London: Prestel.

Howard, J. (2016) *A Thousand Fancies: The Collection of Charles Wade of Snowshill Manor*. Swindon: National Trust.

Inder, P. (2020) *Busks, Basques and Brush-Braid: British Dressmaking in the 18th and 19th Centuries*. London: Bloomsbury.

Johnson, K. (2015) 'Performing Pasts for Present Purposes: Reenactment as Embodied, Performative History', in Dean, D., Meerzon, Y., and Prince, K. (eds.) *History, Memory, Performance*. London: Palgrave, pp. 36–52.

Kidwell, C. B. (1979) 'Cutting a Fashionable Fit: Dressmakers' Drafting Systems in the United States', *Smithsonian Studies in History and Technology*, 42, pp. 1–163.

Langley Moore, D. (1971) *Fashion through Fashion Plates, 1771–1970*. London: Ward Lock.

Leader, D. (2017) *Hands: What We Do with Them and Why*. London: Penguin.

Leis, A. (2013). Displaying art and fashion: Ladies' pocket-book imagery in the paper collections of Sarah Sophia Banks. Journal of Art History, 82(3), pp. 252–271.

Lemire, B. (1984) 'Developing Consumerism and the Ready-Made Clothing Trade in Britain, 1750-1800', *Textile History*, 15(1), pp. 21–44.

Lemire, B. (1991) *Fashion's Favourite: The Cotton Trade and the Consumer in Britain, 1660-1800*. Oxford: Oxford University Press.

Lyons, H. (2024). 'Living "in the bosom of a large and worthy family": Learning to engrave in late eighteenth century London', in Cristina S. Martinez and Cynthia E Roman, eds., Female Printmakers, Publishers and Printsellers in the Eighteenth Century: The Imprint of Women in Graphic Media, 1735–1830. Cambridge: Cambridge University Press.

Malcolm-Davies, J. A., Gilbert, R., and Lervad, S. (2018) Unravelling the Confusions: Defining Concepts to Record Archaeological and Historical Evidence for Knitting', *Archaeological Textiles Review*, 60, pp. 10–24.

Malcolm-Davies, J., Johnson, C., and Mikhaila, N. (2008) '"And Her Black Satin Gown Must be New-Bodied": The Twenty-First-Century Body in Pursuit of the Holbein Look', *Costume*, 42(1), pp. 21–29.

McNeil, P., & Steorn, P. (2013). The Medium of Print and the Rise of Fashion in the West. Journal of Art History, 82(3), 135–156.

McKendrick, N. (1982) 'The Commercializaition of Fashion', in McKendrick, N., Brewer, J., and Plumb, J. H. (eds.) *The Birth of a Consumer Society: The Commercialization of Eighteenth-Century England*. Bloomington: Indiana University Press, pp. 34–99.

Mida, I. and Kim, A. (2018) *The Dress Detective: A Practical Guide to Object-Based Research in Fashion*. London: Bloomsbury.

Mikhail, N. and Malcolm-Davies, J. A. (2006) *The Tudor Tailor: Reconstructing Sixteenth-Century Dress*. London: Batsford.

Miller, L. (2014) *Selling Silks: A Merchant's Sample Book 1764*. London: V&A.

Mire, A. (2019) *Wellness in Whiteness: Biomedicalization and the Promotion of Whiteness and Youth Among Women*. London: Routledge.

Nachman, C. S. (2014). The Queen of Denmark: An English Fashion Doll and its Connection to the Nordic Countryes. In T. E. Mathiassen, M.-L. Nosch, M. Ringgaard, & K. Toftegaard (Eds.), Fashionable Encounters: Perspectives and trends in textile and dress in the Early Modern Nordic World (pp. 133–140). Oxford: Oxbow.

Nimkilrat, N. (2010) 'Material Inspiration: From Practice-Led Research to Craft Art Education, *Craft and Research*, 1(1), pp. 63–84.

Nimkulrat, N. (2021) 'Experiential Craft: Knowing Through Analog and Digital Materials Experience', in Pedgley, O., Rognoli, V., and Karana, E.

(eds.) *Materials Experience 2: Expanding Territories of Materials and Design*. Oxford: Butterworth-Heinemann, pp. 33–52.

Pallasmaa, J. (2009) *The Thinking Hand*. London: Wiley.

Parker, R. (2010) *The Subversive Stitch: Embroidery and the Making of the Feminine*. London: I B Tauris.

Paviere, S. H. (1937). Biographical Notes on the Devis Family of Painters. The Volume of the Walpole Society, 25, 115–166.

Payne, S., Wilcox, D., Pardoe, T., and Mikhaila, N. (2011) A Seventeenth-Century Doublet from Scotland. *Costume*, 45(1), pp. 39–62.

Peers, J. (2004). The Fashion Doll: From Bébé Jumeau to Barbie. Berg.

Petrov, J. (2019) *Fashion, History, Museums: Inventing the Display of Dress*. London: Bloomsbury.

Phillips, N. J. (2006). Women in Business, 1700–1850. Martlesham: Boydell.

Pitman, S. (2022). Dolled up: The material dissemination of dress in early modern Europe. In S. Dyer, J. Halbert, & S. Littlewood (eds.), Disseminating Dress: Britain's Fashion Networks, 1600–1970 (pp. 21–28). London: Bloomsbury.

Polanyi, M. (1966) *The Tacit Dimension*. London: University of Chicago Press.

Priestman, S. H. (1935) *The Priestmans of Thornton-le-Dale and Some of Their Descendants*. Sutton on Hull.

Prown, J. D. (1982) 'Mind in Matter: An Introduction to Material Culture Theory and Method', *Winterthur Portfolio*, 17(1), pp. 1–19.

Rauser, A. (2020) *The Age of Undress: Art, Fashion, and the Classical Ideal in the 1790s*. London: Yale University Press.

Ribeiro, A. (1985) *Dress in Eighteenth-Century Europe, 1715-1789*. London: Yale University Press.

Ribeiro, A. (1995) *The Art of Dress: Fashion in England and France 1750–1820*. London: Yale University Press.

Ribeiro, A. (1998) 'Re-Fashioning Art: Some Visual Approaches to the Study of the History of Dress', *Fashion Theory*, 2(4), pp. 315–325.

Riello, G. (2012) 'The Object of Fashion: Methodological Approaches to the History of Fashion', *Journal of Aesthetics and Culture*, 3(1), pp. 1–9.

Riello, G. (2013) *Cotton: The Fabric That Made the Modern World*. Cambridge: Cambridge University Press.

Riello, G. and Roy, T. (eds.) (2009) *How India Clothed the World: The World of South Asian Textiles, 1500-1850*. Leiden: Brill.

Rosenthal, A. (2004) 'Visceral Culture: Blushing and the Legibility of Whiteness in Eighteenth-Century British Portraiture', *Art History*, 27(4), pp. 563–592.

Rothstein, N. (ed.) (1987) *Barbara Johnson's Album of Fashions and Fabrics*. London: Thames & Hudson.

Rublack, U. (2015). The First Book of Fashion. In U. Rublack & M. Hayward (Eds.), The First Book of Fashion: The Books of Clothes of Matthäus & Veit Konrad Schwarz of Augsburg. London: Bloomsbury, pp. 1–26.

Schmid, S. (2012) 'Mary Berry's "Fashionable Friends" (1801) on Stage', *The Wordsworth Circle*, 43, pp. 172–177.

Schwarz, L. (1992) *London in the Age of Industrialisation*. Cambridge: Cambridge University Press.

Sennett, R. (2009) *The Craftsman*. London: Penguin.

Sheridan, G. (2009) *Louder Than Words: Ways of Seeing Women Workers in Eighteenth-Century France*. Lubbock: Texas Tech University Press.

Simonton, D. (2018) '"Sister to the Tailor": Guilds, Gender and the Needle Trades in Eighteenth-Century Europe', in Ilmakunnas, J., Rahikainen, M., and Vainio-Korhonen, K. (eds.), *Early Professional Women in Northern Europe, c. 1650-1850*. London: Routledge, pp. 135–158.

Smith, S. (2006) *Slavery, Family, and Gentry Capitalism in the British Atlantic: The World of the Lascelles, 1648–1834*. Cambridge: Cambridge University Press.

Smith, C. W. (2013) *Women, Work and Clothes in the Eighteenth-Century Novel*. Cambridge: Cambridge University Press.

Smith, C. W. (2018) 'Fast Fashion: Style, Text, and Image in Late Eighteenth-Century Women's Periodicals', in Batchelor, J. and Powell, M. N. (eds.) *Women's Periodicals and Print Culture in Britain, 1690–1820s*. Edinburgh: Edinburgh University Press, pp. 440–457.

Smith, K. (2012) 'Sensing Design and Workmanship: The Haptic Skills of Shoppers in Eighteenth-Century London', *Journal of Design History*, 25, pp. 1–10.

Smith, K. (2014) *Material Goods, Moving Hands: Perceiving Production in England, 1700–1830*. Manchester: Manchester University Press.

Smith, P. H. (2022) *From Lived Experience to the Written Word: Reconstructing Practical Knowledge in the Early Modern World*. Chicago: University of Chicago Press.

Smith, P. H., Meyers, A. R. W., and Cook, H. J. (2017) *Ways of Making and Knowing: The Material Culture of Empirical Knowledge*. New York: Bard Graduate Center.

Stijnman, A. (2012) *Engraving and Etching, 1400–2000: A History of the Development of Manual Intaglio Printmaking Processes*. London: Archetype Publications.

Stobart, J., Hann, A., and Morgan, V. (2007) *Spaces of consumption: Leisure and Shopping in the English Town, c. 1680-1830.* London; Routledge.

Stobart, J. and Blondé, B. (eds.) (2014) *Selling Textiles in the Long Eighteenth Century: Comparative Perspectives from Western Europe.* London: Palgrave Macmillan.

Strasdin, K. (2023) *The Dress Diary of Mrs Anne Sykes: Secrets from a Victorian Woman's Wardrobe.* London: Chatto & Windus.

Styles, J. (1994) 'Clothing the North: The Supply of Non-élite Clothing in the Eighteenth-Century North of England', *Textile History*, 25(2), pp. 139–166.

Styles, J. (2007) *The Dress of the People: Everyday Fashion in Eighteenth-Century England.* London: Yale University Press.

Styles, J. (2020) 'The Rise and Fall of the Spinning Jenny: Domestic Mechanisation in Eighteenth-Century Cotton Spinning', *Textile History*, 51(2), pp. 195–236.

Sykas, P. (2000) 'Re-Threading: Notes Towards a History of Sewing Thread in Britain'. in Brooks, M. (ed.) *Textiles Revealed: Object Lessons in Historic Textile and Costume Research.* London: Archetype.

Taylor, E. (2020) 'Gendered Making and Material Knowledge: Tailors and Mantua-Makers, c. 1760–1820', in Dyer S. and Smith, C. W. (eds.) *Material Literacy in Eighteenth-Century Britain.* London: Bloomsbury, pp. 151–172.

Thomas, J. (2006) 'Phenomenology and Material Culture', in Tilley, C., Keane, W., Kuechlet-Fogden, S., Rowlands, M., and Spyer, P. (eds.) *Handbook of Material Culture.* New York: Sage, pp. 43–59.

Thompson, E. P. (1967). *The Making of the English Working Class.* New York: Pantheon.

Tobin, B. F. and Goggin, M. D. (2009) 'Introduction: Materializing Women', in Goggin, M. D. and Tobin, B. F. (eds.) *Women & Things, 1750–1950: Gendered Material Strategies.* Abingdon: Ashgate, pp. 1–14.

Van Cleave, K. and Welborn, B. (2013) '"Very Much the Taste and Various Are the Makes": Reconsidering the Late-Eighteenth-Century Robe à la Polonaise', *Dress*, 39, pp. 1–24.

Vickery, A. (1993) 'Golden Age to Separate Spheres? A Review of the Categories and Chronology of English Women's History', *The Historical Journal*, 36(2), pp. 383–414. https://doi.org/10.1017/S0018246X9300001X.

Vickery, A. (1998) *The Gentleman's Daughter.* London: Yale University Press.

Vickery, A. (2009) *Behind Closed Doors: At Home in Georgian England.* London: Yale University Press.

Voth, H. J. (2000). *Time and Work in England, 1750–1830*, Oxford, Oxford University Press.

Walsh, C. (1995) 'Shop Design and the Display of Goods in Eighteenth Century London', *Journal of Design History*, 8, pp. 157–176.

Walz, B. and Morris, B. (1978) *The Fashion Makers*. London: Random House.

Waugh, N. (1968) *The Cut of Women's Clothes 1600-1930*. London: Faber and Faber.

Wilson, E. (2005). *Adorned in Dreams*. London: I. B. Taurus.

Woodyard, S. (2017) *A Milliner's Hand-Sewn Inquiry into Eighteenth-Century Caps ca.1770 to 1800*. MA thesis, University of Alberta.

Zakim, M. (2003) *Ready-Made Democracy: A History of Men's Dress in the American Republic, 1760-1860*. Chicago: Chicago University Press.

Cambridge Elements $\equiv$

# Eighteenth-Century Connections

## Elements in the Series

A full series listing is available at: www.cambridge.org/EECC.

Printed in the United States
by Baker & Taylor Publisher Services